IDENTITY DESIGN®

IDENTITY
DESIGN®

Design the Identity You Need to get the Life You Want

JUDGE FRANK
SZYMANSKI

New York

IDENTITY DESIGN®

Design the Identity You Need to get the Life You Want

Published in New York, New York, by Morgan James Publishing. Morgan James and The Entrepreneurial Publisher are trademarks of Morgan James, LLC.
www.MorganJamesPublishing.com

The Morgan James Speakers Group can bring authors to your live event. For more information or to book an event visit The Morgan James Speakers Group at www.TheMorganJamesSpeakersGroup.com.

ISBN 978-1-63047-435-5 paperback
ISBN 978-1-63047-567-3 eBook
ISBN 978-1-63047-573-4 hardcover
Library of Congress Control Number:
2015917091

Cover artwork by:
Ryan Orlosky

Back cover design by:
JUDGE FRANK Szymanski

Photo by:
Alexis Mitchell

Cover Design by:
John Weber

Interior Design by:
Bonnie Bushman
The Whole Caboodle Graphic Design

Shelfie

A free eBook edition is available
with the purchase of this print book.

CLEARLY PRINT YOUR NAME ABOVE IN UPPER CASE

Instructions to claim your free eBook edition:
1. Download the Shelfie app for Android or iOS
2. Write your name in **UPPER CASE** above
3. Use the Shelfie app to submit a photo
4. Download your eBook to any device

In an effort to support local communities and raise awareness and funds, Morgan James Publishing donates a percentage of all book sales for the life of each book to Habitat for Humanity Peninsula and Greater Williamsburg.

Get involved today, visit
www.MorganJamesBuilds.com

Habitat for Humanity®
Peninsula and
Greater Williamsburg
Building Partner

To Viktoriya, Michelle, and Evan,
for all that you are and all you will be!

CONTENTS

A Word about Judge Frank Szymanski   ix

Acknowledgments   xi

Author's Note   xiii

Preface   xiv

Identity Design (Revealed)   1

Design Questions   27

The Ownership Identity   54

The Challenge Identity   73

Rejection and Failure (The Success Twins)   91

Identity State (What a State You're In)   102

The Kid Identity   118

The Service Identity   134

The Joy Identity   147

The Planning Identity   166

The Now Identity   182

Appendix: Identity Design 49 Questionnaire   195

Bibliography   199

A WORD ABOUT
JUDGE FRANK SZYMANSKI

The people who come before Judge Frank Szymanski are there because they have failed in some way. They are parents who have neglected or abused their children and they are young people who have broken the law in some fashion. Some are there for a minor failure and some are there because they have made choices that have had serious consequences for themselves and for others whose lives they have touched.

I am an attorney who spent almost three years in that courtroom, representing the Department of Human Services in neglect cases. In the course of that time, I have witnessed Frank Szymanski's interactions with many of those people. As a litigator, I have appeared before a number of judges and referees, and I can say without question that I have never known a judge who cares more for those who appear before him, for the victims of their failures, or for the law he is sworn to uphold.

His compassion, empathy, and patience should serve as a model for other jurists. There are no persons whose transgressions are so great that Frank Szymanski won't give them an opportunity to be heard and a chance to change their lives. He treats every person as he would want to be treated in a similar situation. He does not lecture them or pontificate, but, rather, attempts every day to inspire them to do better, to acknowledge their failures, and then to learn from their mistakes so that they may become the best person they can possibly be. Sometimes he is successful but not always. But, even when he cannot change the behavior of a person, he continues to treat them with respect and to encourage them to do better in the future.

I remember one occasion when the evidence compelled him to terminate the parental rights of a young woman who could not extract herself from a violent relationship that was endangering her children. Even after he gave his decision to terminate her rights, he spent a good amount of time talking to her, telling her that she had her whole life in front of her and that she deserved better, that she deserved to have a partner who treated her with respect.

I was moved by that experience, as I was often moved while listening to the judge talk, in his calm and understanding way, to these people who had failed. He would encourage them to try and encourage them to put their failures behind them and to strive for success. I am very glad that Frank Szymanski has decided to share his vision for a successful life with a larger audience. I urge you, reader, to step into his world and be moved, as I have been, by his wisdom.

—**Linda Handren**, Assistant Attorney General for the State of Michigan

ACKNOWLEDGMENTS

This book has been a journey. I am grateful to have found this path. My thanks to Marilyn Angelina, the experienced and dedicated business mentor who first prodded me to write this work. She asked me what I wanted to do. She asked me to assume there were no limits. As a juvenile court judge in Detroit, I was deeply concerned about the trauma I witnessed on a daily basis in my courtroom. The fallout from dysfunctional surroundings and poor role models. Bad circumstances. Bad choices. I had also witnessed phenomenal turnarounds, and brilliant and inspiring resilience. What made the difference? I had come to focus on identity. More than anything else, our identity, who we are, affects everything we do and the life we have. Our identity can change. We can change who we are, and I wanted to work to drive this change. Her words were unequivocal: "You've got to write the book!"

I would like to thank Theresa Wyne for her enthusiastic encouragement and proficient services in editing this work. I would like to thank my wonderful wife, Viktoriya, and our children, Michelle and Evan, for their unwavering support and inspiration. Thanks to my parents, Judge Frank Szymanski Sr. and Lillian Szymanski, and my brothers, Pat, Mike, Dave, Mark, and John, and my sister, Mary Anne. We were raised by our parents in a cooperative, supportive, and loving home, which served as a firm foundation for my current efforts to serve.

I would like to thank my staff at the Juvenile Division of the Third Circuit Court in Detroit, Michigan: Patti Mitchell, Naquay Perry, Karen Hessler, and Officer Diago Walker. Together, we form a team that works to serve our community with dignity and respect in a congenial atmosphere. I would also like to thank all the caseworkers, attorneys, and staff who work with the children and families in our court. Thanks to Linda Handren for her kind words at the beginning of this volume.

My thanks to the team at Morgan James including David L. Hancock, Rick frishman, Scott Frishman, Megan Malone and Angie Kiesling. Thanks to John Weber for the cover design and to Bonnie Bushman of The Whole Cadoodle Graphic Design for interior design. In writing a book about identity design it's great to have the support of the professionals at Morgan James and a great design team.

Thanks to Alexis Mitchell for the professional photography, to Sean Deason for the outstanding logo design, and to Ryan Orlosky for the creative cover artwork. Thanks to Ade Mainor for ongoing technical support and encouragement. And finally, my sincere thanks to the late great John Hughes, my campaign manager, and the voters of Wayne County, and all those who helped me to be elected to serve as a judge in Wayne County Juvenile Court in Detroit. This opportunity has offered me more than I could have ever dreamed.

AUTHOR'S NOTE

While this book is intended to offer strategies for personal transformation in the field of identity design, it is not intended as a substitute for professional psychiatric treatment or professional treatment of any mental or physical condition. I would like to acknowledge that many of the underlying concepts discussed here have been introduced by the universe of great teachers who have preceded me, long before these words were committed to paper. Unfortunately, as I look around I see so much evidence that many of the great lessons of the great teachers seem to be beyond too many of us who are lost in the sea of distractions and contradictions of modern life.

And I have a confession to make. I can't stop thinking about what we're thinking about. Why we think about things the way we do, how we think about things, and then the things that we do as a result of these thoughts. It is my desire to encourage the practice of powerful and generous living. I come to this task in the spirit of humility, hoping to channel what I may in a way that can serve the seekers, those of us who seek to thrive.

This work is offered for anyone interested in redefining themselves, regardless of their philosophical, religious, or theological beliefs. It asks that we recognize the power within us. For those of us who believe in God or a higher power, references to our inner power can be read as a manifestation of this higher power.

PREFACE

You're walking down the street, a street you've walked down a hundred times before, but this time there's something different, something tangible, something you can feel. You're not with anyone at the moment, but you feel connected in a mystic sort of way. You've hit a groove, maybe a favorite melody is streaming through your head, but it's more than that, you feel really comfortable in your skin. It's as if the discussion in your head turned to the questions, "When do I get to be happy? When do I get to live the life of my dreams?," and the answer from the cosmos snapped back at you with glee: "NOW!"

This is what life is meant to be. This is what success feels like. It feels good and it feels free, and you don't need a million dollars or the perfect family or the monster job/car/phone/you name it to have it. In fact, some of those things or the desire for those things can blur, bury, or block it. What you do need is to know who you are and to know that you're on your way. You have an objective, or a set of objectives, that excites you and you're fully engaged. You realize that there is a higher power and you're here for a reason; it wasn't to suffer, it wasn't to worry, it wasn't to envy, and it wasn't to drift.

Ah, and if it wasn't to drift but you feel you've been drifting, what then? We have a unique ability in this world. We may not be as swift as the cheetah, as strong as the bear, or as big as the elephant. We may not have razorlike teeth or eagle eyes, but we have a mind, a functioning brain with the ability to analyze and examine ourselves in a manner unknown in the animal kingdom. It is this gift that has made us the rulers of the world, and it is this gift that offers the key to our development and to our quest for happiness and success. It is also this gift that allows us to imprison ourselves in lives that drift without spark or purpose. Fortunately, there are answers. We need to engage to get them, but they're here. The key lies in our identity. Who we are.

In my position as a juvenile court judge in Detroit, by far the busiest juvenile court in the state if not the nation, I am constantly engaged in the task of remaking the identity of young people and parents who come before the court. While the court is known as the juvenile court, I prefer to refer to it as the court of transformation. I call it that because with teams of dedicated professional administrators, attorneys, counselors, case managers, and others, we work to transform some of the most troubled and dangerous youth in America.

I've worked with young people guilty of everything from stealing a bike to carjacking, armed robbery, rape, and murder. Needless to say, there are some serious identity issues to address here. And while I certainly can't say that we "save" everybody, I can state unequivocally that I've seen some remarkable turnarounds. And while I work to "teach" principles of transformation and identity design in my courtroom, I recognize that mine is the role of a student as much as anyone's as I watch individuals with unheard-of challenges roll up their sleeves, face down circumstances, and change— change who they are and what they're about. It's downright inspiring when you witness this. It affirms what is possible.

There have been millions of words written about how to get what you want and among those words, many of which I have read, are some great ideas. I have included in this book the statement that the objective here is to design the identity you need to get the life you want. With the focus on identity, my objective is to introduce you to, or reinforce in you, the concept that "being" is infinitely more valuable than "having." That no matter what you have, you'll never be satisfied unless you're really happy with who you are. And if you're really happy with who you are, then you're exactly where you need to be.

We all know of people who seem to have everything but their personal lives appear to be a mess. There's an entire industry that has been developed to publicize celebrity scandals and to remind us that while celebrity may bring fame, the fortune part is questionable at best. Celebrity gets you celebrity; it doesn't get you happiness. And as for wealth, you can think about the money, think about the money, get the money . . . but that won't get you happiness either.

Money certainly can make parts of your life more enjoyable, and it can make you feel and appear successful, and the identity work we engage in here is designed to bring it. But the fact is real happiness and real success works inside out. And what's exciting about this is that it means our success, our happiness, and our chance to be who we want to be is at hand. It's not dependent on external forces or possessions. It's not dependent on where we live or what we drive.

We get to decide who we are, and we get to do it now. No waiting. Of course you have an identity right now. And any part of that identity that's not getting you the life you want can be changed. You get to change it and you get to change it now. This minute. I want to impress upon you how immediate this work can be. Once you realize something that changes a belief that you have about something important in your life you, in effect, change who you are.

Now, it might take time for others to notice the change; we're not changing the color of your eyes or your skin. But if you really change something significant, that change is instantaneous. It may take time to manifest or create results in areas of your life, but once you've changed what you believe about yourself, you have changed who you are and the results will flow from there.

Let me invite you to think of this program as a phone booth, just like the one Superman steps into to go from mild-mannered reporter Clark Kent to SUPERMAN. It only takes a shift in perception, a change in belief, to take something that is a weakness in your identity and turn it into a strength, to take you from struggle to mastery. We lose sight of what we're capable of when we get lost in our routines. When we break from the routine, we can see the light of a new world and of a new identity. We are not here to wander. We are here to soar.

The fact of the matter is you can do anything. When I say this, I'm not saying you can outrun Usain Bolt or leap tall buildings in a single bound. When I say you can do anything, I mean anything that matters. We start with the premise that we are all meant to be productive and happy. You don't need to be the world's fastest human to accomplish this. You need to be focused and aware. You don't need to be fast.

There's a movement afoot that has taken the concept of heaven and turned it on its head. Do you believe in heaven on earth? Heaven on earth is the transformational concept that heaven is not some pie in the sky afterlife that follows life on earth for the holy. No, heaven is here and heaven is now. Heaven is the world we create right here through our service to others.

We have within our power the ability to bring peace and joy through action to our community and to ourselves when we deliver our best to those around us. And that peace and that joy, they are meant to be yours now, not years from now when you graduate, when you marry, when you move up or, God forbid, when you retire. That peace and joy is meant to be right here with you, with us, as we make our way.

This book is intended to illuminate this truth and to give you the tools to unlock the doors to who you are, what you want, how to get what you want, and how to "play full-out loud" and enjoy the ride. This program is dedicated to sharing and celebrating the efforts of all who give of themselves to bring heaven to us here and now!

So, thank YOU. Thank you for opening this book and allowing me to share these thoughts with you. I promise to deliver you principles of identity design for your personal and lasting benefit. I guarantee that if you read this book and you apply its principles (meaning you'll have to change, I said CHANGE!), you'll be happier and more powerful and generous than ever. You will redesign.

**Note: Judge Frank is a featured speaker for colleges, schools, church and community groups, professional training and all forms of media on topics relating to Identity Design and social justice. For more information, including free downloads in the field of Identity Design (music, video links, top tips, etc.) or to book Judge Frank for your next event please visit judgefrank.com.

IDENTITY DESIGN (REVEALED)

There is another interesting paradox here:
by immersing ourselves in what we love, we find ourselves.
—Lukas Foss

You have found your identity when you find out, not what you can keep your mind
on, but what you can't keep your mind off.
—A.R. Ammons

Don't be afraid your life will end; be afraid that it will never begin.
—Grace Hansen

The unexamined life is not worth living.
—Socrates

Don't spend all of your time trying to FIND yourself. Spend your time
CREATING yourself into a person that you'll be proud of.
—Sonya Parker

Who do you want to be? If you've never thought about the choice you have in designing your identity, there's no time like now. Identity design is grounded in the concept that "being" is infinitely more valuable than "having." It's the concept that no matter what you have, you'll never be satisfied unless you're really happy with "who" you are. And if you're happy with who you are, what you have becomes secondary. Authentic being is your source of infinite power. Would you like to design your thoughts and actions, your essence, who you are? Welcome to *Identity Design*®.

What Is Identity?

What do you want? Good question. But it's not the first question . . . who do you want to be? That's the question we need to start with. The secret to life lies not in what we have or what we want to have, but in who we are and why we're here. Identity has been defined as the qualities, beliefs, etc., that make a particular person different from others. We need to pay close attention to our beliefs because they define us. We can survive or we can thrive. We can manage to get by or we can excel. We can live. We can dream. More than that, we can live the life of our dreams.

Are you living the life of your dreams? You can be. You should be. What does it take to do so? I believe the problem for most of us is that when we start talking about the life of our dreams, the first thing we think of is "the money." What about the money? Yeah, what about the money? The money to give us more freedom to do what we want. But we need to focus on who we want to be rather than what we want to have. The fact is we tend to confuse what we have with who we are. We want things. No secret there and no shame in that. That's wonderful. Wanting things drives ambition, and ambition leads us to get things done.

However, an oversized focus on what we don't have interferes with our sense of well-being. It steals our joy. We want what we want, and once we get what we want, what happens? We start wanting something else. This pattern replays in a perpetual cycle. If we're going to live a life of joy, the life of our dreams, we need to find our joy where we stand with who we are. We need to start living the life of our dreams now! We need to recognize that we can be who we choose to be, regardless of what we have.

It's confounding to see young people in my courtroom who have risked their liberty by stealing a phone, a pair of shoes, or a car. What real value can be achieved by taking these things? Yet here they stand, day after day, week after week, in my courtroom. These acts reflect faulty values and a misshapen sense of identity. These individuals need to redefine themselves and establish their being in a way that would make such acts unthinkable.

We confuse what we've done and what people have said about us with who we are. What we've done is just that, something that we've done. We can choose to let that define us if we want to, but we don't need to. It's not a definition of who we are. It's just something we've done.

The fact is good people do bad things. Good people do harmful things. None of us is perfect. None of us goes through life without making mistakes. Sometimes bad mistakes. Those mistakes can only define us if we let them. This is true even in the most extreme case. Someone who has been convicted of murder can be called a murderer, but only they can choose whether they live their life as a murderer or as someone else.

In fact, I know a man named Darryl Woods who was convicted of murder after someone was killed in a drug deal. Darryl was present and was convicted as an aider and abettor. He is serving life in prison for his offense. While he has accepted responsibility for his actions, he has moved beyond them. Though he has received the ultimate sentence, life in prison, he has redefined himself as a counselor and has taken on the task of making sure other young people don't make the same mistakes he did.

While serving his sentence he has joined with some of his fellow prisoners, as well as Jeff Allison, a corrections official, and warden Anthony Stewart of the Michigan Department of Corrections, to establish the Youth Deterrent Program. Young people come to the Detroit Reentry Center, where Darryl is serving his sentence, and Darryl and his colleagues talk with them about what it means to be facing the ultimate consequences for a criminal act. The conversations are frank and personal, and I've seen young men talk of their most difficult troubles with the Youth Deterrent Team, men they've never met before. Darryl Woods has not let his mistake define him. He's using these most unfavorable circumstances to enable him to help others. He's changing the world from a prison cell.

I have titled this effort *Identity Design* and design we will, but there is also a good bit of discovery involved in this process if it is to be relevant and meaningful. You and I, and all of us, are different physically, emotionally, and spiritually. The identity that will bring you peace and joyous living will be different from mine, but we can use the same tools of self-discovery and design to uncover our core selves and mold ourselves into the "who" we want to be.

So, what if you could change anything you wanted? Your height, weight, facial features? Your hair color? (Well, that one's easy enough.) If you could change your appearance in any way, would you? How? What would it do for you? A few years back there was a popular program called *Extreme Makeover* in which people underwent plastic surgery to obtain dramatic differences in their appearance. The highlight of the program was the "reveal" in which people were reintroduced to their family and friends after being gone for months while they underwent their physical transformation. The compelling part of this climax of the program was the change in confidence displayed by the participants as they reveled in their new look.

The fact is they had the same set of memories as before, the same experiences, but through this process they had come to see themselves in a new way. What changed for them on the outside helped change them on the inside. The fact is you can make every bit as dramatic a change, and more so, without a dime of plastic surgery or lip gloss or dental work. Your identity can be reshaped, remodeled, and redefined by you. You just need to accept that this is within your power and get to work. This book is intended to serve as a comprehensive program for this work. You're free to think of this as *Extreme Makeover: The Inside Edition*. With the inside edition, we're taking on our thoughts head-on.

Please turn to the appendix and take the Design 49 Quiz at this time. You'll need less than ten minutes of uninterrupted time to complete this simple quiz. DO THIS NOW.

Welcome back. The purpose of this quiz is to engage you in the process of thinking about what you're thinking about, and to start considering the kinds of things that are at work in the shaping of your identity. We will address some of these items directly as we proceed

You may or may not have read anything about personal development before. Whether you have or haven't, whether you've changed anything as a result or not, this is different. Why? Because it has to be. The life you have at this very moment is a result of your current identity, your current beliefs about yourself, and your current beliefs about the world around you. If you want to change the life that you're sitting on at the moment, the one you're experiencing, you're going to have to change some things about what you believe about yourself and the world. **You're going to have to change what you think about what is possible, but more than that, you're going to have to change what you think about what is PROBABLE.**

There's a difference between thinking of what could happen and what will happen. We're not talking about predicting everything that will happen. We're talking about recognizing your ability to handle everything that will happen and your ability to shape what will happen. If that sounds like power, you've read it right. This is a book about power and your ability to recognize and cultivate it—your ability to design for it.

When we talk about identity design, we're not here just to get more willpower so we can exercise more, lose weight, or finish a project. It's time to redefine. It's time to redefine ourselves in a way that these other things we're after start happening simply because we've redefined ourselves. We're talking about addressing the underlying causes of why we see ourselves as we do so we can change in a fundamental way. We're talking about enlisting our subconscious (the part of consciousness that is not currently in focal awareness) as a front line ally.

Sports psychologists discuss the champion mindset. Many agree that this is what is most critical to a champion's success, much more so than raw talent. So too, there's no reason we can't change our mindset and learn to think as champions do, to move with confidence in our abilities, to be champions in our own lives. You might not be able to hit a tennis ball like Roger Federer or to play football like Tom Brady or Joe Montana, but why can't you think like they do? The fact is you can.

Tom Brady has won three Super Bowls as an NFL quarterback and three times has been named Super Bowl MVP. Yet, before this success he enrolled at the University of Michigan and was ranked seventh on the depth chart at quarterback. Interestingly enough, he hired a sports psychologist to work on his mindset as he struggled for playing time at Michigan before eventually earning the starting role. Something told him he needed help. He needed to change his mindset. You can study and adopt role models, learn their thinking patterns, and adopt them for your own. Successful living takes a certain mindset and if you're not there, you soon can be. You soon will be.

When you start a car you put the key in the ignition, turn it, and step on the gas. You may have done this thousands of times without thinking about it. We are going to use this act of ignition as a symbol of what is to come. You are going to add consciousness to this formula. This program is designed to get you thinking more consciously about what you're doing, and even more than that, to get you thinking about what you're thinking, which then impacts what you're doing.

Starting a car is the first act of control you exercise over your vehicle when you go for a drive. Nothing happens without ignition. Ignition is in your control. As the driver, you determine what happens. Think of the car as your world. You are going for a drive. You are in control. And if you're like me, sometimes you need to be reminded of this. We will discuss this further later on, but for now, understand that this program is designed to empower you to acknowledge the power you have and to exercise it in a way that makes you productive and happy.

In my work as a juvenile court judge, I receive evaluations from clinicians about the young people who have committed crimes and the parents who have neglected or abused their children. Invariably, there is a common denominator in these reports: low self-esteem.

Once we find a young person responsible for a crime or a parent responsible for neglect or abuse, we take jurisdiction and hold regular review hearings geared to supervise the rehabilitation of the young people and the parents before us. At these hearings, I ask people to analyze the choices they're making and the kind of life they're getting as a result of these choices.

This is an inquiry we all need to be involved in, because in any area of our lives where we're not getting what we want, we need to start with looking at the choices we're making and seeing how those choices are shaped by our identity. **Changing our identity will change our choices.** When we see ourselves in a powerful way, we act accordingly. However we see ourselves affects our choices, and our choices bring us the life we experience.

Whether you've given it much thought, you've been engaged in identity design since before you were born. Inside the womb, with the development of your nerves, your spinal cord, and thalamus, you had all of the parts necessary to experience pain by week twelve. By week seventeen, you could dream sleep. By week twenty, you could not only hear, you could recognize your mother's voice. These are your first experiences, and your identity has been shaped by the sum total of your experiences, conscious, and unconscious since your conception. This shaping is an ongoing process that includes everything you think, everything you feel, everything you do, and everything you experience.

And here is the first truth you need to embrace: "Identity Is King." Just as all of your experiences and thoughts and actions shape your identity, so too your identity imposes itself on every breath you take. Your identity is the seen and unseen pilot at the controls of your body, your mind, and your soul. Your identity is the arbiter of your actions and your reactions, your emotions and moods, your ups and downs and your in-betweens, what you hope for, wish for, want and fear, how you look and feel and taste and touch, what it takes to make you cry and laugh, where you go when it rains, and whether you choose to stick with it, give up or move on. **Your identity defines your place in this world and your connection to it. Sacred.**

Our identity defines us infinitely more than our red hair, brown eyes, broad shoulders, or big hips. Those are just things that people see. Our identity is who we are. How we see ourselves, that's our identity. Do we see ourselves as happy, productive, successful? More? Less? What? How do we see ourselves right now? How is this affecting how happy we are?

Our identity is not how other people see us. It couldn't be. A hundred different people can see us a hundred different ways. That would be terribly schizophrenic. For our purposes here, we are working on an inside job. Admittedly, the way other people see us CAN have a major impact on how we see ourselves, and in most cases, it does. But that's subject to change. The fact is that successful people have such a strong self-identity that they can go against the grain, go against the consensus of popular opinion, go on and do things that most people don't consider possible.

Successful people can do this because they know what they're about and they refuse to be enslaved by what other people think. Does that sound like a powerful way to be? Columbus was able to sail off to the edge of the world because he realized that what he believed mattered more to him than what anyone else believed. The power of the universe is in all of us. Our job is to find our place, our identity, and line up with it.

You don't need to have a unique belief like Columbus had to lead a great life. But you need to believe in yourself. That belief along with direction and discipline can take you anywhere you were meant to be. What is it about self-belief? Why are some people filled with it while others are full of doubt? Ah, one of the great mysteries. **The fact is whatever your level of self-belief is right now, you need to**

send it a message. The message is: SUBJECT TO CHANGE. Hear this message because you cannot complete this program without adopting new insights that will shift the balance of power of your self-belief. This is needed, unless you've already done so, in which case I expect you are already living the life of your dreams.

Make no mistake about it. **Nothing happens without belief.** If you want to do something, but deep down you don't really believe you can, or you will, how can you expect to do it? The fact is you can't. You need to believe. **Believe and be.** When we talk about changing beliefs, we're talking about changing who you are. We're talking about changing what you see, feel, hear, and say. Your beliefs dictate your focus. You might say if it's that simple, I'll just change what I believe and I'll get what I want. It is and it isn't. Saying that you have a new belief is not the same as having a new belief. One of the primary purposes of this book is to provide you with information and activities so you can see for yourself that your beliefs really can change and that you have the absolute power to change them.

The realization that how we see ourselves serves as our identity comes with good and bad news. The good news is we can do something about it. And that's what we're here for. The bad news is, for many of us, this identity of ours is being shaped by others. We're just following trends. We're buying into the "messages" that surround us. The fact is if we're not fully engaged in the design of our identity, we are at the mercy of everyone else's influence. Our identity is, in effect, being designed in default mode.

The world is chock-full of spoken and unspoken messages that are itching to imprint themselves on us. We have advertising that pushes us to buy something. Even if we don't "buy" the product, the message is still received and can impact our view of who we are and what we should have. We have a flood of other messages and cues that come from friends, family, coworkers, and others and they leave their impression. For example, if everyone around you complains about the weather, as a result of this influence, guess what . . . you're likely to complain about the weather. This gets you nothing but adds to your identity as unhappy and as a complainer. Between complaints about the heat, the cold, the wind, the rain, the clouds, and on, and on, I sometimes am left with the impression that some people are only satisfied with the weather ten to twenty days a year. On those days when the weather is beautiful, I wonder if people who regularly complain stop to remark on the beauty.

This may seem like such a simplistic example, but it's here to make a point. Are we here to complain about the weather? I don't think so. And if we follow the "crowd" on these points, where does this lead us? We'll use the term "crowd" here to designate the collective influence of those around us, either personally or through some form of media.

One of the golden rules of message analysis is "consider the source." So, is the source some person or organization that we have come to respect? If so, why? If not, how should that affect our receipt of the message? Maybe we should just ignore it. Maybe we should consciously shut it down. If we're going to create and live in the identity we need for the life we want, we're going to have to be very aware of everything that impacts our identity, everything that can shape our view of ourselves. It all starts with awareness because if you're blind to something then you just can't do anything about it.

For example, let's turn to the question of financial success. In a dynamic book called *The Spirituality of Success*, Vincent M. Roazzi points out that 93 percent of Americans never achieve financial independence. That's right, 93 percent. And from whom have we have received our "instructions" regarding what we need to do to achieve financial independence? If we're learning from the 93 percent who have never achieved it, what confidence can we have that their message will lead us to where we want to be?

In his eulogy for Robert Kennedy, Ted Kennedy quoted his brother, "Some men see things as they are and say why. I dream things that never were and say why not."

Everyone has an imagination. Are you using yours? When was the last time you looked into your future and smiled? The word "imagine" means to form a mental image. **The word "imaginization" has been crafted to indicate that we can shape our world and our place in it through our thoughts.** That means we can choose to interpret every event we experience, everything we see, hear, feel, touch, and taste in any way we like. And we can imagine any kind of future we wish.

The future we're after won't occur if we don't take action, but our actions are guided by our thoughts. **Imaginization is power.** We all have it. As children we were masters of it. Many of us were simply never introduced to the idea that we can use it to shape our lives. We unconsciously adopt habits, patterns of thought, and behavior that rule our lives and limit our outcomes. The bottom line is it doesn't have to be this way.

You have likely heard the expression "You are what you eat." However, the greatest impact on our daily well-being is our thoughts. **In actuality, "you are what you think."** What you think determines what you eat. We have all seen two people in similar circumstances respond in completely different ways. The difference? Attitude. Some people respond to every challenge with positive "can do" energy. They believe in themselves and in their ability to ultimately be successful in the face of all obstacles, and they act accordingly. They can "see" things will turn out if they persevere. Other people lack this self-belief and allow challenges to prevent them from reaching success. Without self-belief people fail to form concrete plans for success, or simply give up when challenges emerge.

What Do You Say When You Talk to Yourself?

Let's start to take a look at who we are by looking at some self-talk statements (thoughts that we may have), both positive and negative.

- I am always late.
- I am always on time.
- I am disorganized.
- I am efficient.
- I can never make up my mind.
- I am a slow starter.
- I need direction.
- I don't like to look foolish.
- I like to make plans.
- I sabotage myself.
- I don't follow through.
- I'm not good with computers.
- I'm not good with directions.
- I'm full of energy.
- I can't get a good night's sleep.
- I'm healthy.
- I hate getting up in the morning.

- I'm generous.
- I'm happy.
- I never have enough money.
- I'm stuck.
- I'm a leader.
- People like me.
- I have great charisma.
- I'm polite.
- I'm not a very good reader.
- I'm not good with numbers.
- I don't like taking chances.
- I don't like to stick out in a crowd.
- I'm lucky.
- I'm dynamic.
- I'm creative.
- I'm generous.
- I'm loving.
- I'm decisive.
- I'm a great public speaker.
- I'm motivated.
- I'm energetic.
- I'm electric.

Self-Talk Activity

Now, those are some possibilities. Let's see what you come up with on your own.

I'm _____

I'm _____

I'm _____

I'm _____

I'm _____

Now, let's take a look at some of these statements. Where do they come from? Positive or negative, these thoughts are not universal. For the statements that you feel apply to you, think about why you feel they do. Also, think about whether they empower you or disempower you. Think about whether they make you a stronger or a weaker person.

We're out to change or unload any disempowering thoughts, and the first step to doing this is becoming aware of what they are. We're also out to reinforce and emphasize our empowering thoughts. **When it comes to self-talk thoughts we need to adopt a "keep it or kill it" attitude.** We can't afford to keep the negative ones if we're going to be successful in our redesign campaign.

There are three questions to ask ourselves about whatever beliefs we have: What do I believe? Why do I believe this? Does this belief give me more power or less power? (If the belief gives us less power, we have a fourth question to address: What am I going to do about it?)

Let's go back to the car analogy. Every time you have one of these negative thoughts, you're adding sludge to your engine, your mental engine. Why would you do that? The more sludge you have, the more difficult it is to operate efficiently. We want to "run clean" or as cleanly as possible if we're going to get the life we want.

Let's take another look at some additional statements, two sides of the coin so to speak, from an article called "Can Positive Thinking Really Improve Your Life?" by Jonathon Wells at AdvancedLifeSkills.com. Jonathon gives us a look at how we might view something from a negative standpoint versus a positive one.

Negative Spin	**Positive Spin**
I've never done it before.	It's an opportunity to learn.
It's too complicated.	I'll tackle it from a different angle.
I don't have the resources.	Necessity—the mother of invention.
There's not enough time.	Let's re-evaluate some priorities.
There's no way it will work.	I can learn to make it work.
It's too radical a change.	Let's take a chance.
No one communicates with me.	I will start the conversation.
I'm not getting any better at this.	I want to give it another chance.

You can see the difference here in the two approaches. One set of thoughts is a virtual mental roadblock. The other set is an invitation to a world of possibilities. **To be powerful, we need fewer roadblocks and more possibilities.** We are working to enable ourselves, not to shut ourselves down. We have enough obstacles to challenge us without erecting our own. As you adopt a confident "can do" identity, you'll find your spin echoing more and more positive. This is not an option to get the life you want. This is a must.

Life So Far Activity

We're ready now for our first piece of in-depth interactive work in this design project. This is where we find out how serious you are about this. How you apply yourself to this task and the tasks that follow will determine what you gain from this project; it will determine whether you will, in fact, accomplish the changes you seek. If you fail to participate in doing these tasks, you reduce this book to mere information. Information without action is worthless. Do you really need more worthless information? The whole point of this is to get you where you want to be, and if that's going to happen then you're going to have to move. You're going to have to do something, and there's no better time to do something than now. I'm making a big deal out of this because, for one thing, it's necessary, not recommended, but *necessary*.

And for another thing, I have a confession to make. I can remember many times reading a book that dealt with some aspect of self-analysis or self-improvement and getting to the point where the author would say, "Now, get out your pencil and paper and write out a list of this or a description of that." And I can remember being in a comfortable reading position, enjoying the reading and saying to myself when I read an instruction like this, "Well, that sounds good. I'll get to that later," and, sure enough, that would be as close as I'd get to doing what was suggested. I offer this confession not to serve as a model for you. I have cured myself of this failing, and now when I am presented with an activity, I take it on. I offer this to admit my guilt and to get you to act. Are you in?

So, we're going to start by declaring it's over. Your life. Over . . . done. Over and done. Right now. And now you have the task of writing your obituary, your life story. While you could go on for days, or hours, at this, a half hour to an hour is sufficient. We don't need every detail but we need the gist of it, the basics. There should be some focus on "being."

In other words, what kind of "identity" have you brought to your life so far? This is not the flowery eulogy version, the version of life that we hear in church where people feel compelled to say only the good things about someone. We need the basics, the good, the bad, and the ugly. And if you're going to emphasize anything it should be the bad and the ugly. More on this later, but for now, it's time for paper and pencil, and put the book down, and do this now because I expect you won't read another word beyond this paragraph until you've done it. You can start by saying, "He died with a great book in his hands." Just kidding! Now let's have it, your story if you keeled over from a heart attack and your life ended right now. Pencil and paper, give it to me. DO THIS NOW.

Welcome back. So, you've been honest in your portrayal and now you need to size up "your life so far" as you've described it. Who did you describe? What identity did you identify? What are the strengths you see? What are the weaknesses? What has held you back from meeting your potential? The point is not to beat yourself up over any shortcomings you see. The point is to become aware of them so you can do something about them.

Admiration Activity

Here is our next step. Vincent M. Roazzi presents a fun and illuminating identity activity in *The Spirituality of Success*, and we're going to use it here. Pencil and paper again. Take five minutes and list the people you most admire. They can be alive or dead. It's not necessary that you've ever met them. Just make a list of all of them you can think of in the next five minutes. DO THIS NOW.

Welcome back. Now, take your list and next to each name put an adjective that best describes why you admire this person. Thus, you would say "wise" rather than wisdom. And avoid generalities like "cool" or "awesome" that don't really tell us anything in particular. Focus on descriptive specifics such as "confident," for example. If you want to use more than one admirable quality for a person, go ahead, but use one-word descriptions of that quality. DO THIS NOW.

Now, take each adjective from your list and combine them into a single list of adjectives. Look over the list carefully. DO THIS NOW.

Voilà. There you are. The list identifies the qualities you most admire. And your list of names gives you models for each quality. The list is you. You and your aspirations. Since you identified these people and these traits as ones that you admire, combining them gives you the person YOU want to be.

You could look at this list and say, "Well, there are times when I haven't been like this, when I haven't been brave, or bold, or creative, or dynamic." Well, haven't we all? Even the most dynamic and inspirational leaders in history had faults and doubts at times, just the same as we do. They persevered. They learned. They grew. They wrapped their identities closer to their core values— the same as we can. This is where we need to start turning that brilliant ability that we all have to be critical of ourselves from a negative into a positive. From the ability to beat ourselves up over our shortcomings into the ability to identify when we are thinking or acting out of line with our core values and draw ourselves back in line with the "who" that we aspire to be. **It's not perfection we're after. IT'S PERSISTENCE.**

Acknowledgment Imaginization
Now, let's take another look at our list. While it's no doubt a good one, we may have missed a few characteristics, so let's give ourselves a chance to add to it. Think of any other adjectives that you might have missed that are important to you.

I have an activity to help with this. Close your eyes, breathe in and breathe out slowly, four or five times, and picture yourself walking. You can choose whatever setting you like. Perhaps you're on a beautiful beach, warm weather with a perfect breeze, the sun dodging in and out of beautiful white clouds. As you stroll down the beach, you see people gathered ahead, and as you approach, you feel about as good as you could feel. It's one of those days of which you could ask nothing more.

Now, as you begin to walk through the crowd, you may recognize friends, family, teachers, colleagues, and others. You are walking confidently and they are all acknowledging the greatness within you. They are commenting to each other as you walk by. They are saying, "He's so kind or brilliant, so this or so that." They are commenting on all of your characteristics. Take time as you walk to listen to what they're saying about you. Hear everything you would like to hear them say. Listen to them say it as they say it with deep and sincere belief and enthusiasm. And then they begin to say these things directly to you, in a way that leaves you grinning from ear to ear. You could almost think they were there to flatter you, but you can hear the ring of truth in their words. This is what it feels like to be at home and at peace with your pure character. This is what it feels like to have the unique qualities of your character acknowledged for what they are, a gift from the highest power in the universe. Add any new characteristics that you hear to your list. DO THIS NOW.

This is a great activity for you because not only does it help you identify any qualities or characteristics that you may have missed in our prior activity, it also gives you a chance to experience what it feels like to be this way and to have people recognize that THIS is who you are. When you visualize—or as I like to emphasize by creating the word "imaginize"—something in such a powerful way, your mind accepts it as if it actually happened, so that mentally, spiritually, and emotionally, you get the benefit as if it actually *did* happen.

When Harvard University researchers tested subjects with a brain scanner, they found that seeing a picture of a tree and imagining a tree activated the same parts of the brain. One study showed that people who imagined themselves performing a certain exercise, without actually doing it, still increased their muscular strength. In our "acknowledgment imaginization," it's as if these people *did* say these things about you BECAUSE THEY WERE TRUE.

The more often you repeat this activity, the deeper this feeling connects inside you and takes over your brain. It's like that pilot that was sitting at your controls is being kicked out by the new guy who is getting all of the praise for the great qualities he possesses. And it feels pretty good. In fact it feels great. This is identity design. (Cue music here for dramatic effect!)

This activity is a kick-starter too because many of us spend too much of our time in a place where the face of change is rarely seen. A place where dreams die, and progress is measured in inches, if at all. Familiar territory. It's a place where the things that we do get us more of what we already have rather than the things that we lack, the things that we really want. A place where the familiar overshadows the unknown. A place we call the "comfort zone." I'm not talking about the "zone" in which athletes, craftsmen, professionals, and artists find themselves totally absorbed and at the peak of their powers. I'm referring to a place of comfort and a place where there is little need to grow or change. Once we "settle" in here, we find inertia holding us in and holding us down.

Self-imposed limitations become more and more powerful with the passing of time. If we want to live the life of our dreams, we have to transcend our comfort zones, get outside the box, and spread our wings. We have to learn. We have to shed our skins, our routines, our habits. **If you're not exactly where you want to be right now, you have to move. And moving within your comfort zone simply will not do it.**

Train Wreck Imaginization to Shatter Negativity

Our next activity is an opportunity to use our imaginization to pulverize negative thoughts. It's designed to put you in command of dealing with the negativism you've experienced. It's a specific visualization you can use anytime you like, and you can repeat this when you face any new negative statements. While this imaginization comes with very specific imagery, you can design your own dynamite/destruction scenario with any details you like. You need to take this on when thoughts are dragging you down. Read the description, then close your eyes, and experience it for yourself. DO THIS NOW.

We're going to close our eyes and breathe in . . . and breathe out . . . and breathe in . . . and breathe out . . . and breathe in . . . and we're going to imagine we're at a train station with open top gondola cars along the track. We want to picture an extremely powerful engine at the head of a set of these cars. We're going to load in all the negative thoughts, all the negative comments, and negative circumstances that we can think of into these cars. We watch them get lifted by a crane into each of these cars and we fill as many cars as we wish. Think of all of these negative thoughts and just load them in, anything and everything that's held you back or caused you to doubt yourself in any way.

Once this is complete, we're going to sound the signal and watch the train pull out of the station. You can wave goodbye if you like because this train won't be returning. We're going to watch as it picks up speed pulling its freight across the rails, surging faster and faster until it's headed out along a flat open plain with nothing to slow it down and the throttle wide open. It surges along, and now it hits top speed and continues to blister along the tracks. Up ahead in the distance, there's an end to the plain where a sharp cliff with a drop-off of thousands of feet awaits. But, no matter, the throttle remains wide open as the wheels sear along the rails at matchless speed.

Onward and ever closer to the cliff, closer and closer and still closer until it would be too late to stop, regardless of intent, until now the lead wheels of the engine run out of track and fly clear off the end of the rails. Yet sheer momentum carries it out two full car lengths above the gorge before gravity can begin to wrest it from its forward momentum and start to pull the engine downward. All the cars behind it, with their cargo of all the negative thoughts and comments you could ever recall, are pulled along and pulled into the descent until the end of the train clears the track. Now, it's all caught in freefall for thousands of feet with the cargo spilling from its position. Everything hurtles to the ground, falling and falling until it all smashes to pieces.

You can survey the damage if you like. You could send in a team of the finest salvage experts, but be assured that everything in that train and the train itself has been shattered beyond repair. If you've lived your life in the shadows of doubt under the weight of claims of your own inability to thrive, prosper, and be happy, whether those claims are self-inflicted or otherwise, they hold no more power. All of that negativity has been shattered. While you may have some question of what lies ahead, recognize this: . . . as for the past . . . that train has left the station . . . you are free.

Should you choose to design your own activity here, remember the more dramatic, the better. You can't overdo it.

Life to Come Activity

Now that we've sent the limitations over the cliff with the speeding locomotive, and we've identified the characteristics that we value, and we've imaginized our stroll on the beach acknowledged by all, we can proceed to jump ahead to the finish. We're going to take a leap of faith. We're going to use our pencil and paper again and our fully liberated "imaginization."

This time we're going ahead in time to our "real" imaginary end. Not the one that takes place today, as we did a few pages earlier, but the one that will come eventually to us in this life. For those of you who believe as I do that this life and these "bodies" we inhabit are merely temporary forms for our energy and our spirit, we are going to nonetheless use the expression "the end" to refer to the end of our earthly life.

So, for our purposes here, we are at some time in the future determined by you. You need not have a specific date; a general time frame is sufficient. (I expect you will select the somewhat distant future. After all, I think you would like to have time to experience the joy of living with your newly discovered and newly designed identity coming out of your work here.) At this future time, you have now gloriously passed on. You are to write your obituary or life story from here forward.

You can embrace this as an emotional experience. Let your thoughts flow. You should feel free to proceed in whatever fashion works best for you and allows your thoughts to flow freely. Just keep the focus on what is to come and not on what has been up until now. And know that this is your movie. In this imaginization episode, you write and edit the script, direct the performance, play the central role, and frame the cinematography. You control everything . . . just like you're going to control your life.

Again, we don't need every detail. We are looking for the highlights. Specific events can be included as you wish here, but the real heart of what you have to include is the "identity" part of your story. Who did you live your life as from here on? Did you live as the person you have been up until now? Or did you fully embrace your aspirations? Did you live up to all of those great things that people said about you as you walked the sand in the cooling breeze? Did you let go of the expectations and the standardized limitations of others?

This is the rest of your life we are dealing with here, so you want to make it compelling and thrilling. You want to conjure up the kind of life that will make you excited to get up each morning. As you write this, picture it all. Picture it and feel it. The only limit is your imagination, and at this stage, that shouldn't be any limit at all. If you find yourself thinking, "Well, that will never happen," LET THAT THOUGHT GO! Truth is stranger than fiction. I've seen this in my courtroom many times. Here we go. Back to the future. DO THIS NOW.

Welcome back. Activities such as this have been linked to significant increases in happiness. If there's anything, let me repeat, ANYTHING, that you don't like about how your life turned out in this scenario, just pull out your eraser or hit your delete button now and rewrite accordingly. We will call this the "life to come" activity. This is your turning point. You see NOW the good to come. The more often you perform this activity, the more you align your consciousness with your destination. This is your life, this is your show from here on out. Rock on and let it roll.

And while we have taken the long view here by looking at your full "life to come," the fact is this "look back" activity can be done for the month to come, the week to come, the day or even the hour. Set yourself up for a good week by writing your way back from seven days ahead as you just did with your life. Talk about the great things you've done, and feel your sense of accomplishment at having done them. This activity puts into focus what is important for you to do and acknowledges you for actually having done it. It's a double whammy.

When the week is over, you can read your account and see how it matches with what really occurred. And if it didn't fully measure up, don't be dismayed. Maybe you missed the target. We all do from time to time. The fact is you will have HAD a target. Think of the days and weeks and months that you've wandered along without a target. You're more productive with one. After you look back at your week, you can pull out your pen and look forward to the next week to come. The more that you do this, the better you become at setting, marking, and hitting your target. Power and confidence will follow. Nice work.

It has been reported that we may have as many as 70,000 thoughts per day; that's an average of forty-eight per minute (though I'm not quite sure I can think that fast!). This brings us to three central questions for the implementation of identity design: How many of those thoughts are we controlling? Or managing? Or focusing? More control, more management, and more focus is the direction we're headed. Every ounce of thought we reclaim will take us in the direction we need to go. Let's look at taking this on one minute at a time. Can you spare a minute a day to redefine your identity? Beautiful!

The 7/60 Mad Minute Identity Design Plan

What can you do in sixty seconds? **Sixty seconds of pure focus is a dynamic force at your command that can redefine your identity.** The discipline to activate this force is available to anyone who chooses it. I have developed a seven-day schedule to cultivate essential thought patterns to support your personal identity design. The underlying concepts will be presented later in this program and the full breakdown of the plan will follow, but for now I would like to introduce you to the sixty-second-focus concept and give you something work on.

You're going to go on the clock for sixty-second intervals at least once a day, seven days a week, ergo the 7/60 plan. We call these "mad minutes," minutes in which nothing else matters. If you need to know where the name came from, I borrowed "mad minute" from my daughter Michelle's first grade arithmetic class. They have to complete a full page of arithmetic problems in five minutes or less, and they progress through levels, and as Michelle has told me, these are mad minutes. The concept generates a sense of urgency and accomplishment in first graders, not much differently than what we are doing here. I'm only giving you a minute so the urgency is compounded by a five to one ratio. This is a test. Do you have the focus of a first grader? You're going to need it.

If you have a stopwatch for this, that's great, because starting and stopping it can serve as an anchor for these one-minute sessions, but you can also use a secondhand on a watch or clock. The timing adds a level of formality and focus, but is not intended as a limit. If you like what you're doing and desire to continue, then go ahead and continue for as long as you like. The key is to engage for at least one minute in which nothing else matters and nothing can stop you. If your daily schedule permits you to use a given time of day, that's fine, and if not, you'll need to find that minute for yourself, but make sure you do. If you get to the end of the day without having engaged in this, then take a minute and do so.

Initially, you will take this minute and check in on your awareness. When you check in, think of what you've just been thinking about. Think of what you're doing and why you're doing it, what you're feeling and why you're feeling this way, and the connection between what you've been thinking, feeling, and doing. You are checking in. One of the things we need to do more effectively if we are going to live more effectively is to be "present," to work in the "now." This one-minute activity is designed to do just that, to get you into the now for at least one minute a day.

Before you close this minute down, there's one more thing. Think of something you are grateful for. This only takes a few moments. If you are grateful for someone in your life who has been loving and supportive, think of something specific that they've said or done that you are thankful for. And the next time you get the chance, thank them. Or maybe you're simply thankful for the way something worked out. This can be something big or small, something in your career, your relationships, or even your recreational activities, anything. A moment of gratitude will shift your attitude. We're taking a moment, a minute, a "mad" minute, to exercise the control and the focus we've been talking about. We are directing and managing for this minute. We are not reacting or drifting. We are asserting, analyzing, and then thanking. Gratitude is powerful; it's a booster shot for your immune system and your self-image.

On alternate days, we'll shift the minute of focus to service. For one minute, be of service. Be in giving mode. Concentrate on doing something to make someone feel good. This can be done by complimenting or acknowledging someone in a special way. This can best be done face-to-face, but can also be by phone, text, email, or any other form of communication. You can also physically help someone with a task of some sort, even if it's something they would normally do themselves without help.

For this to be true service, you should expect nothing in return. You want to simply experience the joy of unbridled giving and the personal power that you possess in making someone else's life better. We will be discussing the value of gratitude and service further, and these focus minutes will make these essential matters part of your everyday life in a way that makes them even more valuable to you. The specific attention you apply will bring additional dividends as you assert and acknowledge your ability to direct and control.

You can schedule Monday, Wednesday, and Friday as service days and Tuesday, Thursday, and Saturday as check-in/gratitude days. For now, we'll use Sunday as a rest day. Don't underestimate the power of a minute. Over time, that minute of command will start influencing the rest of your day, and as I've indicated, we will introduce variations to impact the most decisive elements of identity design. We will redefine.

There's no better time to start this practice than now. Take a minute; take a mad minute right now for your benefit. Start with a check-in/gratitude mad minute. DO THIS NOW.

Welcome back. Hopefully, you haven't gone completely mad! As you can see, when you focus, a minute is actually a substantial amount of time. Unfortunately, much of the time we are just coming and going and doing, merely "reacting." You just started pushing the needle in the other direction, the control direction.

Identity Design and the Concepts to Come

I'd like to provide a preview of what is to come. Here are some thirty-second capsules of the concepts you will work on to develop the identity you need to get the life you want in upcoming chapters. I have introduced the concept of Identity Design, and I will follow that with our trip through the elements of that design.

Design Questions

Questions, questions, questions. Why are questions so important? Because they shape the most important discussion we ever have—the one we have with ourselves. The right questions are rocket fuel for growth. The wrong questions stagnate and victimize us. If we are going to control the conversation in our head to get the life we want, there's no better place to start than with the questions we ask.

The Ownership Identity

Who's in charge . . . of your life? When you look at your life and the results you're producing, the life that you're living, you have to make a choice as to who you believe is responsible. If you blame others, you surrender your life to them by putting them in charge. By adopting an ownership identity you embrace personal responsibility for your life. You assert your power to create your results. Who owns your life? You do.

The Challenge Identity

How do you respond to challenge? High achievers identify challenge as a gateway, a springboard to where they want to be. We need to recognize that challenge is a never-ending part of our journey, and that big challenges can teach big lessons and fuel major growth. As we develop this attitude, we thirst for and thrive on challenge, and good things happen as we recognize that we don't control everything that happens around us. We control our response. That bears repeating: We control our response.

Failure and Rejection (The Twin Engines of Success)

Have you been rejected? Are you a failure? If so, you're in good company. Everyone who has ever accomplished anything has failed along the way. They simply realize that this is part of the process, and they keep going. In some cases, they keep failing over and over again until they get what they want. Like a child learning to walk, falling down means you're taking risks and working outside your comfort zone, and that's where growth happens.

Identity State (What a State You're In)

What is "state"? State is defined as a mode or condition of being. We have powerful states and powerless states. If we want to maximize our power and effectiveness, we need to seize state control. This means managing emotions and mastering moods. You can do this because your emotions and your moods are just that—yours! State control relies on awareness and discipline, and let's not forget practice.

The Kid Identity

Kids have their own way of looking at things, and we can learn a lot from them. In many ways they're better at "living" than grownups. They haven't "learned" all the adult ways to look at things. They haven't become saddled with grownup prejudices, and stereotypes, and inhibitions, and worries. This frees them up to take on life in ways that many adults never do.

The Service Identity

Why do we serve? Service is the ultimate action for personal fulfillment. Research shows serving affirms our connection with others, builds our self-esteem by establishing our value, and makes our hearts grow stronger. We become healthier and happier when we serve, when we give, when we love. The more we give, the more of us there is to give. If you want to make a friend, change the world, feel alive, serve somebody.

The Joy Identity

Are you happy? Joy is our birthright. We should be happy most of the time. Happiness is a skill. It's also a choice. We can find our joy where we stand with who we are. As we recognize our blessings, we position ourselves for joyful living. The world and our circumstances have been uniquely designed for our personal growth and benefit. As we live and we give, we have reason to rejoice—now!

The Planning Identity

Do you have a plan? We can't expect to get anywhere if we don't have a plan. People without a plan get used by people who have one. Your life is meant be just that—YOURS. To have an effective plan, you need to decide who you want to be, where you want to go, and how you're going to get there, and take action to make it happen. Your life is in your hands when you have a plan.

The Now Identity

Is there a better time than now? Who cares? This is now. The more we make of it, the better off we are. Now is like the fairytale "Beauty and the Beast." It's what we choose to see. Look for the beauty and see the beauty, or look for the beast and see the beast. The beauty of now is that it gives us whatever we bring to it. The baggage of the past and the hopes and fears of the future become meaningless when you embrace the present moment completely. Some of us are so busy running scripts of endless chatter about everything (at the rate of forty-eight thoughts per minute) that we've made the present moment a foreign land. Why not . . . just . . . let it be . . . now . . . wow.

You are now engaged in designing the identity you need to get the life you want. Congratulations! As you pat yourself on the back, remind yourself that while we still have a lot to do you are exactly where you need to be.

Every day going forward will be a growth experience for you, and each day you will continue to redefine who you are. You are taking on your thinking with a vengeance, driving your transformation. The beauty is that while this work never ends, this work is the game itself. You're playing now whether you know it or not. So, claim your joy on the road with who you are and where you are right now, knowing . . . that this . . . is only the beginning.

And as we move on, we need to think about the questions we need to ask . . .

○⊏⊐ POINTS TO REMEMBER: ⊏⊐○

- Are you living the life of your dreams? You can be. You should be.
- If you want to change the life you're sitting on at the moment, you're going to have to change what you think about what is PROBABLE.
- Changing our identity will change our choices.
- Your identity defines your place in this world and your connection to it.
- The fact is that whatever your level of self-belief right now, you need to send it a message. The message is: SUBJECT TO CHANGE.
- Nothing happens without belief. Believe and be.

- The word "imaginization" has been crafted to indicate that we can shape our world and our place in it through our thoughts. Imaginization is power.
- You have likely heard the expression "You are what you eat." In actuality, "you are what you think."
- When it comes to self-talk thoughts we need to adopt a "keep it or kill it" attitude.
- To be powerful, we need fewer mental roadblocks and more possibilities.
- It's not perfection we're after. IT'S PERSISTENCE.
- If you're not exactly where you want to be right now, you have to move if you want to get there, and moving within your comfort zone simply will not do it.
- Sixty seconds of pure focus is a dynamic force at your command that can redefine your identity.

DESIGN QUESTIONS

We thought we had all the answers, it was the questions we had wrong.
—Bono

It is easier to judge the mind of a man by his questions rather than his answers.
—Pierre-Marc-Gaston, duc de Lévis

The quality of our life is reflected in the quality of the questions we ask.
—Anonymous

No man really becomes a fool until he stops asking questions.
—Charles Steinmetz

To solve any problem, here are three questions to ask yourself:
First, what could I do? Second, what could I read? And third, who could I ask?
—Jim Rohn

I never learn anything talking. I only learn things when I ask questions.
—**Lou Holtz**

Who are you?
—**Pete Townshend**

Questions, questions, questions. Why are questions so important? Because they direct what we think about and how we look at things. We all have a continuous conversation in our heads—the mental chatter that goes on daily, minute to minute, second to second. To be successful in the field of identity design, in order to design the identity we need to get the life we want, we need to seize control of this conversation. I'm not suggesting we can control every thought that crosses our mind. What we can do is analyze thoughts and our reaction to them.

What do we do with these thoughts? We have three types of thoughts in relation to our identity. Those that are neutral, those that are harmful to our identity, and those that empower us. If we're not living the life we want, we need to reframe the balance of these thoughts so that we are maximizing the empowering thoughts and minimizing the damaging thoughts.

There's no better place to start than with the questions we ask. The quality of our life is reflected in the quality of the questions we ask. We can't hope to find the answers if we don't ask the questions. We can't hope to know ourselves, to find our identity, if we don't ask who we are. Let's look at some basic questions regarding our identity.

Who am I?

This is the essential question. **If we are not happy most of the time, we either don't know who we are, or we know who we are but we are not being true to ourselves.** If we don't know who we are, or we know who we are but we are not being true to ourselves, we have a follow-up question we must ask:

Who do I want to be?

The two questions cited above address the most fundamental thing about us: our identity. Our identity provides a reference point for what matters. Once we focus on who we are, who we were meant to be, **when we define ourselves, we**

can begin to meaningfully ask what's relevant to our lives. Once we understand what's relevant, we can measure how well we are staying on task, how true we are being to our identity. Understanding and focusing on our identity doesn't mean we become single-minded or that we lack an array of interests, but it does give us a critical perspective to maintain priorities.

The Three Lies of Identity

There are a number of things that cloud our judgment, that make it difficult to get to the heart of who we are. There's so much misunderstanding as to what makes us who we are. There are three big lies of identity. These are sinkholes, craters of quicksand that swallow our identity. Unfortunately, this happens and we don't even realize it. These lies are so pervasive and infiltrate our thinking so completely that if we were to consider the "battle" for our identity, it's as if we lost the battle without firing a shot because we didn't see the enemy coming. We didn't know there was anything to shoot at or to guard against. Without an examination and an understanding of these lies, we may think we're fine, or at least okay. In reality, these lies hamstring our ability to thrive. Let's take a look at the big three lies of identity.

Lie Number One: You Are What You Have

The first big lie of identity is that you are what you have. This, in some ways, is the biggest lie of all, and it is perpetuated by the combined massive effort of all the major corporations of the world that want you to believe that you and your happiness are defined by what you have so that you will do everything in your power to buy what they want to sell you.

You are not defined by what you have, by where you live, what you drive, the phone you use, or the clothes you wear. Allowing yourself to be defined this way simply means you've bought somebody else's dream. It means you've bought their dream that you are defined by what they want to sell you. This is madness, yet the propaganda machine that is behind this lie is immense, and it includes all the trillions of dollars that have ever been spent on advertising.

This lie is the underlying reason for so-called celebrity endorsements. Why do we have celebrity endorsements? Because we've been herded into thinking we need to be like the rich and famous, and to be like the rich and famous, we need to have what the rich and famous have. We have celebrities who endorse products that they would never even use. How much Coca-Cola or Pepsi do you really think any of these celebrities drink each day? A single celebrity contract can be worth millions of dollars to the celebrity because companies see the value in having you associate what they want to sell you with that celebrity. And do you know what the biggest problem with this is? It works! That's why people who get paid millions of dollars a year to hit a baseball, shoot a basketball, or throw a football, make even more millions of dollars each year telling you what they drive or what they wear.

This lie is not limited to advertising. It's everywhere. It dominates the conversation of who we are. The "entertainment" industry is full of "messages" about the value of being rich and famous. There's an underlying inference that life begins when you've "made it." We get so attached to possessing things that some of us risk everything just to have more than what we have now. Our "wanting" pulls us out of balance.

I recently was asked to address a group of teenagers at the Detroit Juvenile Detention Facility. JDF is a temporary placement facility for young people awaiting trial or a long-term placement. I was there as part of the face-to-face program that is a joint effort of our US District Attorney's Office and the Wayne County Department of Child and Family Services. I wanted to drive home the fact that we create nothing but problems for ourselves when we define ourselves by what we have.

So, I brought with me my "show and tell" bag, a midsized roller duffle. I pulled out a brown paper grocery bag and labeled it as an identity bag. The problem is that some of us are risking not only our liberty, but our integrity, for the contents of the bag. I set the bag on the gym floor in front of one hundred-plus kids. The problem is too many of us confuse who we are with what's in the bag or with what is represented by the contents of the bag. So, what exactly was in the "identity" bag? What was in there that I had recently locked someone up for on a third offense in an unarmed robbery case? You can take a guess.

After giving them a moment to ponder exactly what was in the bag, I pulled out a pair of Reebok Retro Kamikaze 1 Mid basketball shoes. Their unique design reminded me of black forest cake with medium-blue neon icing drizzled in a zigzag affair across the top. Delicious looking, if such a cake ever existed. I found it ironic that Reebok named these particular shoes Kamikazes after the Japanese pilots who flew suicide missions against the US Navy in the Pacific theater in World War II. We now have young people killing each other for gym shoes. Life is not about the shoes. We shortchange ourselves when we allow it to be.

Unfortunately, high-end sneakers have become status symbols. This is a perfect example of the problem. I understand this young man didn't think he'd get caught, but the fact is he had attached himself to owning something that wasn't his. We could refer to this as "attachment disorder." (I am not referring to the more traditional use of this term, which is a label for those who fail to form normal attachments to primary caregivers during early childhood.) While most of us don't actually steal to get things we want, it's our wanting, our wishing, that does the damage. Anytime we allow it to dent our personal sense of exhilaration in even the slightest way, we are surrendering to this attachment disorder.

Unfortunately, the indoctrination of lie number one starts early. When children are in grade school, they start sizing each other up based on what they wear. In many schools, if you don't have the right look, the right clothes, you don't have access to the "in crowd." You're just not going to be accepted or popular. If you go to any mall in America, you can find kids in "uniform." A pair or group of teens or pre-teens wearing the same style, cut, colors of shirts, jeans, shoes, and jackets. Different cliques may have different looks, but within a clique, the regimentation is remarkable. It's all about fitting in with the right brands. Our possessions are simply things that we own, and when we consider the fact that we don't take them with us when we die, we need to acknowledge that we're merely renting these things that we think we "own."

Think of your most treasured possession. Now, consider that you might lose it in a natural disaster or in some other way. What difference would it make as to who you are? Now, consider something that you don't have, something that you really want but you don't have. If you actually had it, how much difference would it make as to who you are? What I'm insinuating is that both of these questions have the same answer: not much. Not Much? No, the real answer is "nothing at all."

Think about how much time you spend thinking about things that you want. I'm not suggesting that there's anything wrong with people wanting things. Wanting things drives ambition and gets things done. The problem with the massive emphasis on acquiring and having things is that we let it interfere with who we are. When the "wanting" takes over our "being," this is destructive and disruptive to our identity, and it steals our joy. How much time do we, you and I, spend thinking about things that we don't have? Things that are not available to us because we don't have the money? Consider how this affects your self-image. The biggest lie of identity is that you are what you have, or even worse, what you don't have.

Lie Number Two: You Are What Other People Think of You

The second big lie of identity is that you are what other people think of you. No, this is not who you are either. No two people experience anything or anybody in precisely the same way. You don't take on a new identity every time you meet someone new. People have opinions of you, of us, understood, but that's not who you are. Letting those opinions override your sense of identity is just as big a mistake as allowing yourself to be defined by what you have.

Here's the problem: It's a giveaway. You are not what others think of you, and you can't afford to think that you are. Identity is your sense of who you are, not somebody else's. Letting someone else define you surrenders power, surrenders control. If you're going to live the life of your dreams, maximum control is essential. The more that we maintain control and responsibility, the more powerful we are.

In order to make this point when I spoke at JDF, I pulled a box out of my show-and-tell bag. The box was about one foot long on each side and a foot deep, and I attached a paper on each side with one word in large type. The first three words read, "What will they," and the fourth word was covered with a sheet taped over it. When I asked for the word on the last side, a number of individuals were able to correctly guess the last word. You can take your guess now.

The last word was "think," as in "What will they think?" To emphasize the point, I placed the box on my head for a moment. The fact is we need to get the what-will-they-think box off of our head. We need to think out of the box, so to speak. That's not where life is. We won't be able to find our dreams in the what-will-they-think box.

Worrying about what others think is one of the biggest obstacles people have to living the life of their dreams. I have two words for you here, two special words: "peer pressure." This is the influence or force of others that affects how we think, what we do, or what we wear. I have seen kids get involved in terrible crimes as a result of basic peer pressure. A "friend" wants to carjack somebody, or to break into somebody's home. Carjacking carries a maximum sentence of life, and the max on first degree home invasion is twenty years. After accepting guilty pleas on these cases, I ask individuals why they did what they did. I get answers like "I wanted to fit in." So, someone who wants to fit in risks these dire consequences by joining in.

When it comes to what we think we might do, we wonder, "What if I try this and it doesn't work out the way I planned? What will they think?" Well, what will "they" think? And who cares? You and I are not here to live within the limited expectations of others. Think of a child learning to walk. He just keeps falling down until he gets it figured out. He is oblivious to anyone's opinion as he stumbles along the learning curve. He's focused on walking, not on what others think. This is another example of the value of staying in touch with our "inner child." We may not like to be seen as a failure, but a failure can be very liberating. The bigger, the better. Once you fail and you realize it's not the end of the world, you're free to move on, without the baggage of worrying about a blow to your self-image. You've already taken that shot.

There's actually a great deal of negative synergy between lie number one and lie number two because we tend to think that what people think of us is based on what we wear or what we have, or even more often, what we don't have. So, here we go again. This compounds the effect of lie number one, but we can sidestep this pitfall by remembering that we are not what we have and we are not what others think of us. To paraphrase John F. Kennedy in our context here: Ask not what others think of you; ask what you think of yourself.

Lie Number Three: You Are What You've Done

The third big lie of identity is that you are what you've done. False. What you've done is just that, something that you've done, and while it will affect what other people think of you, what you've done is not who you are. We've all made mistakes, some of them bigger than others. Letting our mistakes define us is like piling one mistake on top of another. Why would we do that?

At JDF, I had a visual aid to make this point also. I brought in a rearview mirror I bought at an auto parts store. I had it passed through the audience, and I asked everyone to hold the mirror in front of them as if they were in the driver's seat of a car and to make a mental note of two things that they could see in the mirror. After allowing the mirror to make its way through the audience, I asked everyone to think about what they saw in it. Then, I asked where everything was that they saw in the mirror. Of course, everything they saw was behind them, the same place everything that we have ever done is—everything we've ever done is behind us. And everything that has ever been done to us, or said to us, or about us, is behind us.

Let's consider a couple of examples of how this plays out. A tennis player is playing a hotly contested match with an opportunity to break serve early in the third set. He plays an aggressive point and forces a short lob from his opponent, which gives him a chance to hit an overhead. This is a shot tennis players relish because it's a chance to win the point in commanding fashion with what is known as an overhead smash. Yet even at the professional level where hitting a smash is like making a layup in basketball, players occasionally miss this shot.

For purposes of our discussion, let's say that's exactly what happens here—the player misses the smash by driving the ball beyond the court. Thus, he loses the point. While he can say it's a point he should have won, the fact is he didn't. He made an error, which every professional player has made at one time or another. He needs to put it behind him to play the next point. But that's not always what happens. He might choose to obsess over the error and let what happened continue to play out in his head, interfering with his ongoing performance as an inner voice tells him he's a "loser" or a "choker."

Or consider someone who is dieting. They're at a party and they have a piece of cake. Now, they've "gone off their diet." They could see this as a minor setback and recommit to their diet, or they could see themselves as lacking the ability to follow through on their diet and return to the eating habits that caused them to be overweight in the first place. These are examples of piling one mistake on another.

In the history of man, no one has ever been able to change something they did yesterday, or an hour, or even a minute ago. You are no different. Strangely enough, we spend a lot of time obsessing about things we've done as if we could. This may not come as a total shock, but I'd like to point out just how unproductive this is. You can't do anything about the things that you've done except learn from them. And if it's appropriate to apologize, then apologize, but recognize that that does not change what you've done. I'm sure you've heard this before: "What's done is done." We need to start acting like it.

Think of that rearview mirror in your car. Everything you can see is behind you, and every moment as you drive forward, more things show up in the mirror as you travel down the road. A car driving down the road is like time marching forward. The moment you're living right now will be behind you in the very next moment, just like all those things that are showing up in the mirror as you drive down the road. Letting our past define us is like driving through life looking in the rearview mirror. Is that any way to drive? Is that any way to live? We need our rearview mirror for backing up. In life, we don't get to back up. "Time marches on," as they say. No backward marching. Unless you're Superman and you can fly through time.

There is an Internet project sponsored by the Alan Alda Center for Communicating Science that sponsors something called the Flame Challenge. The program is an annual contest to explain science concepts in an understandable way to an eleven-year-old. The 2013 challenge was to explain "What is time?" The winner, Nick Williams, defined time as "Forward Movement." Everything moves forward, and man developed a way to keep track of this forward movement and called it "time." This forward motion will never change, never stop, and can never be reversed (except in comic books and science fiction movies). This explanation can help us and eleven-year-olds everywhere to focus on moving forward now and always.

What you've done is not who you are. It's who you were. Rather, it's a reflection of who you were at the time you did whatever you did. Each time we learn something from what we've done, we are, in effect, reinventing ourselves with new knowledge and new experience. There are people who don't really change. They make the same mistakes over and over again. They exist. They live with a limited view of themselves and what they are capable of. But it's not because they can't change. It's because they choose not to. They find it easier to stay within their comfort zone with "what they know." Many people tend to hold on to what is familiar even if it's not what they want. The comfort of familiarity, even miserable familiarity, can be a powerful draw.

Change is a choice you can make, just the same as choosing not to change is a choice you can make. **We need to recognize that we are in the "choosing" business.** Mistakes need to be learning experiences, not crippling experiences. You are not what you've done; that's who you were. If you don't like what you've done, you can change who you are because what you've done does not define you.

Certainly there are good things, even great things, that you've done, and you should be proud of these things. They also don't define you, but they should build your confidence. Just don't remain fixated on some past accomplishment. Life is about moving on. Even the great artists of the world didn't dwell indefinitely on their achievements. At the height of their popularity, the Beatles were recording two to three albums of original material a year, an unheard of amount of productivity for such a popular act. The albums *Beatles '65, Beatles VI, Help!* and *Rubber Soul* were all released within twelve months' time. *Magical Mystery Tour* was released six months after *Sgt. Pepper's Lonely Hearts Club Band.* The Beatles were writing, arranging, recording, and performing at such a pace, there would have been little time to sit around congratulating themselves on the great music they were creating. They were busy looking for the next melody as soon as they finished whatever they were working on. Artists like this enjoy the process more than the results. Think of what we can learn from this example. That "being" and "doing" are more important than "results."

When we turn our focus to who we are and what we do, we attain a level of power and satisfaction that transcends any mere result. At this point, results will follow as a result of the concentration of power. Good or bad, the things you've done do not define you. Learn from your failures, take confidence from your successes, but define yourself in the moment. "Be" who you choose to be.

How do you see yourself now? Now that we've looked at the three big lies of identity, we can start to see how wide open we are to defining ourselves any way we choose, and how important it is that we make this a conscious choice. **We need to "choose" our identity, separate and apart from what we have, what others think of us, or what we've done.**

We need to be aware that the questions themselves shape the answers we find. The questions shape the conversation. In shaping the conversation, the questions shape our identity. In fact, our identity is dictated by the questions we ask. Let's look at a range of questions we might ask ourselves on various topics.

Exercise
- Why can't I get time to exercise?
- How do I feel about exercise?

(Do you see the difference here in where your thoughts might go in relation to these two questions on the same topic?) How about these questions?

- Don't I feel great when I exercise?
- I haven't exercised in five days. What am I going to do about it?

We all know exercise is beneficial. All the research says it is important for our physical and mental health. Which of the questions above can we expect to lead us to be successful in getting more of it?

Money

- How come I never have enough money?
- How do I feel about money?
- Don't I feel great when I apply myself and earn value for my efforts?
- I haven't earned what I'm capable of. What am I going to do about it?
- Why do I seem to always want to spend more than I have?
- Why is it I always seem to have enough money for what I need?

Education

- Why do I go to school?
- What does my education mean to me?
- How do I feel about learning?
- What do I like learning about the most?
- Why would I ever want to stop learning?

As you can see, there are questions that suggest an obvious answer. There are questions that are open-ended. There are questions that are neutral, questions that are damaging, and questions that are empowering. **Our questions shape our internal conversation and our conversation shapes our identity.**

There are also victim questions. The all-time classic is "Why me?" We've all asked ourselves this at one point or another. There is no power that comes from this question. **We need to kill all of the victim questions.** This question is full of self-pity and despair. We are not here to be pitied. And I don't mean to belittle any of us who find ourselves asking this question, especially in moments of extreme grief. It's understandable. It's natural. But we have to work to get past it as soon as we can because there is no power in asking it.

And what about the classic "Why can't I" questions?

- Why can't I lose weight?
- Why can't I quit smoking?
- Why can't I find a better job?
- Why can't I find the love of my life?

Why? Why? Look at the bloody question. The question itself is one of the great negative affirmations of all time. If you say, "Why can't I lose weight?" you are affirming the fact that you can't. The fact that you are asking yourself this question is an admission that you can't do something. You might as well be saying to yourself, "I can't lose weight, I'm not exactly sure why but I know I can't."

Now, let's look at what is fact and what is not. The fact is you've wanted to lose weight and you haven't. That's the operative fact. And, in fact, people lose weight all the time, so what makes you special here? You need to recognize that whether you're talking about losing weight, or quitting smoking, or getting a great job, there is a world of difference between the words "haven't" and "can't." The point is language is important. Words are important. If you want to run with the big dogs, you're going to have to speak the language, and the language of the big dogs doesn't include "Why can't I . . ." questions.

However, they might very likely include questions such as "How will I . . .?" A "How will I" question could imply that you WILL do something, and that's the kind of question we should be asking. Successful people know enough to ask empowering questions. It is their nature. Their identity leads them to ask empowering questions.

Identity
- Who am I?
- Who do I want to be?
- What do I want?
- How do I need to change to get what I want?
- What am I going to do differently today?
- What am I going to learn today?
- Where am I going today?
- Let's look at a couple of critical questions for self-awareness:

- Who is influencing the way I look at myself?
- What is influencing the way I look at myself?

We have to be mindful of how much there is to these questions. A common practice is measuring ourselves financially against others. Society places a world of importance on what we have compared to what others have, and there are always others who have things that we don't have. As stated previously, this is the first big lie of identity. If this is where our focus is, then we are setting ourselves up for a lifelong tail-chasing pursuit. As soon as we get what we are focused on getting, our focus changes to getting something else that we don't have. And it happens so subtly that we don't even realize it.

Satisfaction comes in brief episodes without any real sense of joy. This is not joyful, powerful living. This is the serial distraction of modern day consumption. We need to take a hard look at how our income and our possessions are affecting our identity. We are not our income. We are not our possessions. Those are just things we have. As we stated earlier, "being" is infinitely more valuable than "having." We need to ensure that "having," or more specifically "not having," is not getting in the way of our "being."

We've all had special experiences in our lives that were critical to shaping our identity. These can come at any point and accumulate as we grow older. These can be positive and negative experiences. Some positive experiences could include specific academic achievements, being hired on for a job you wanted, getting a special promotion at work, falling in love, a special achievement in sports or a hobby, the birth of a child, etc. Some negative experiences could include the loss of a job, a breakup with a boyfriend or girlfriend or a divorce; witnessing or participating in domestic violence or violence of any kind; a traumatic physical injury or illness; the death of a family member or a close friend; contact with law enforcement as result of any criminal action, etc. We can understand ourselves better by working to analyze these experiences and our reaction to them. Let's start by identifying at least three positive and three negative experiences in our lives and analyzing, as best we can, the impact these experiences had on us. We can start by identifying the experience by saying, for example, "When I was seventeen . . ."

Next, let's ask our critical questions about the experience.

- How did I feel during this experience?
- How did this experience affect me?
- How did this experience shift my identity or the way I feel about myself? Was I different before and after the experience?
- Do I look at this experience differently now than when I experienced it?
- What were my thoughts about others who were involved in the experience?
- Did I take responsibility for my actions in this experience?
- If I had this experience today, would I react differently? If so, how? Why?
- What did I learn as a result of this experience?

DO THIS NOW.

You might have some additional questions about a given experience that should be asked and, if so, good for you, that's a sign that you are really taking on this aspect of identity design. Add them to the above questions, and then go to work on answering them. In doing this, you're breaking down significant stages in your development. You're breaking down what happened, your reaction, and the impact of it all. These are experiences that have impacted your whole life, and while I'm sure you've thought about them a great deal, you may have never fully analyzed them this way. You can list your experiences, and then tackle them in alternating fashion by starting with a positive experience and then addressing a negative experience, or vice versa. The beauty of alternating your discussion is that it reinforces your understanding of life as an evolving journey with ups and downs and ins and outs.

While I have asked that you identify experiences as "positive" and "negative," these are only general categories as I have described them above. You may find in your analysis that what most people consider to be a negative experience, such as the death of a loved one, has turned out to be an experience that has caused you to redefine yourself in an extremely positive way. You may find that what most people consider to be a positive experience has caused you to redefine yourself in a negative way, or has driven you in a direction that you now consider to be unproductive or unhealthy in some way.

Don't be surprised by this. Life often works this way. In looking at the way negative experiences can be positive, my favorite expression is **"What doesn't kill you makes you stronger."** When faced with challenges, this is one of the first things I work to think of. As far as positive experiences becoming a negative influence, you might find that some achievement gave you an inflated view of your own importance and caused you to be less respectful of others.

These are defining moments. The question is how do you define them? Allow your analysis to take you where it will, and be open rather than defensive in your analysis. The goal is understanding, not some scorecard that leaves you in the best possible light. If we are going to redefine our identity, we need to work with tools of change, but we need to understand what we can about how we came to be where we are in the first place. The only way we can do that is to be honest with ourselves.

While you are free to share this analysis with friends or family, there is no requirement that you do so. However, you may find it helpful to ask others about what they remember of your actions in these experiences you've identified. With their different perspective, they might provide you with some insight you've missed. So this may take some time, but this could prove to be some of the most revealing work of this project, so don't rush it. Pencil and paper, identify three or more positive and negative experiences, and answer the questions set forth above and any others that you consider important regarding these positive and negative experiences in alternating fashion. DO THIS NOW.

You can look at every part of your life and ask a new set of questions to move you in a new direction. Let's look at key areas of life and some questions to address.

Physical
- How do I rate my physical health on a scale of one to ten?
- What are my strengths?
- What are my weaknesses?
- If I continue to act as I do now, what can I expect my body to be like in ten years?
- What action can I take to improve my physical health?
- What benefits can I expect if I take action to improve my health?
- What will be the benefit to others if I improve my physical health?
- Is my current path sustainable? (In other words, if I continue as I am at this time, will I maintain an acceptable level of physical health?

Mental

- How do I rate my mental health on a scale of one to ten?
- What are my strengths?
- What are my weaknesses?
- If I continue to act as I do now, what can I expect my mind and my overall attitude to be like in ten years?
- What action can I take to improve my attitude and mental health?
- What benefits can I expect if I take action to improve my attitude and mental health?
- What will be the benefit to others if I improve my mental health?
- Is my current path sustainable?

Career

Note: Since we have a separate set of questions relating to our financial circumstances, this career section should focus on achievement and job satisfaction.

- How do I rate my career satisfaction on a scale of one to ten?
- What do I like about my career?
- What do I dislike about my career?
- If I continue to act as I do now, what are the reasonable expectations for my career in ten years?
- What can I do to improve my career?
- What benefits can I expect if I take action to improve my career?
- What will be the benefit to others if I improve my career?
- Is my current path sustainable?

Recreational

- How do I rate my recreational life on a scale of one to ten?
- What are the highlights?
- What are the lowlights?
- If I continue to act as I do now, what can I expect my recreational life to be like in ten years?
- What action can I take to improve my recreational life?
- What benefits can I expect if I take action to improve my recreational life?
- What will be the benefit to others if I improve my recreational life?
- Is my current path sustainable?

Financial
- How do I rate my financial health on a scale of one to ten?
- What are my strengths?
- What are my weaknesses?
- If I continue to act as I do now, what can I expect my financial health to be like in ten years?
- What action can I take to improve my financial health?
- What benefits can I expect if I take action to improve my financial health?
- What will be the benefit to others if I improve my financial health?
- Is my current path sustainable?

Social (Friends and Family)
- How do I rate my social life on a scale of one to ten?
- What are the highlights?
- What are the lowlights?
- If I continue to act as I do now, what can I expect my social life to be like in ten years?
- What action can I take to improve my social life?
- What benefits can I expect if I take action to improve my social life?
- What will be the benefit to others if I improve my social life?
- Is my current path sustainable?

Spiritual
- How do I rate my spiritual life on a scale of one to ten?
- What are the highlights?
- What are the lowlights?
- If I continue to act as I do now, what can I expect my spiritual life to be like in ten years?
- What action can I take to improve my spiritual life?
- What benefits can I expect if I take action to improve my spiritual life?
- What will be the benefit to others if I improve my spiritual life?
- Is my current path sustainable?

The last question in each series asks if our current path is sustainable. In other words, can we maintain as we are in each of these areas if we simply keep doing what we are doing?

You could choose to examine other areas that hold particular interest for you, but the areas identified above cover core fields of your life, and if you rate yourself highly in all of these areas, it would be difficult to imagine that you would not be deeply satisfied with your life. Feel free to add or improve the questions offered (and to forward your suggestions for the next edition).

By starting out with a rating question, we've borrowed a concept from the business world that "what gets measured, gets managed." And while it's natural to be thinking we're after tens all around, that's fine as an objective, but not at the price of current happiness. That would violate the principle this work is founded on, that we don't need everything to be the way we want it in order to be happy.

Life is a process, a journey, and in a vibrant life, we are always growing or expanding so even if we reached a ten, we would want to keep going to eleven (like the guitar amps in Spinal Tap). Two of my primary interests are music and tennis. These are fields that defy mastery. There is always something new to learn about composition or production in music. New hybrid instruments and software are being created as we speak. While the game of tennis is not developing at the same breakneck speed, the mind/body connection and focus that the game requires is subject to never-ending improvement. So, I have a couple of activities that I thoroughly enjoy while I know I'll never approach perfection at either. That's not to say I never get frustrated, but more and more, I realize when I do that I am just getting in my own way. I need to recognize what we've stated here. It's a growth process. As Stuart Smalley, the Al Franken character from *Saturday Night Live*, would say, "I'm okay with that."

We've looked at some core fields of life and some questions we can ask to evaluate how we're doing and where we're headed with our current actions. Having done so, this is a good time to look at one of the ultimate life-defining questions. We all have different roles in life. We have different hats that we wear. For example, I'm a judge, a father, a husband, a brother, a friend, a singer/songwriter/musician, a tennis player, a surfer, an Olympic bobsledder (just kidding), a coach, a writer, a speaker, a big game hunter (just kidding again), and on, and on. But, while these are all things that I do, they do not define me.

The question is "What does define me?" What defines you? Sure enough, you have a number of roles yourself. But if you only had one sentence to define yourself, to tell someone what is most important about you, to convey your essence, what would that be? Take a moment to write out your current working definition of you. This is not a list of things that you do or roles that you play. This is who you are. This should tell us something essential about why you're here. What is your mission? If we are going to develop the ability to live the life we want, we need to adopt a position of personal power. Our definition and our mission should reflect this. Write out your personal one-sentence definition. DO THIS NOW.

Welcome back. You now have a definition. It may change but you've given yourself a reference point. Think of this reference point as the North Pole for your compass. Are the things that you do pointing north? Are they consistent with your definition of yourself?

When I think of my personal definition, I like to refer to it as my seven-second miracle. In seven seconds I can define who I am, the source of my power and my reason to be, that which connects me to others in this world. This may sound fairly ambitious for a seven-second statement, so be it. **I've established the following definition for myself: "I am a spiritual power source created by God to help others live the life of their dreams."**

This definition includes a declaration of power, and of the source of that power, and a reason to be that goes beyond myself. It's a declaration of service. It's a declaration that allows me to claim joy, my joy, now. Here and now. The beauty here is that anytime I catch myself thinking about something that I want that I don't have, I can think of this definition and remind myself that these other things that I want are just noise. They're not essential to who I am and why I'm here. If they turn up, that's fine, but again who I am is more important than what I have. This definition reminds me of that.

When I lose a tennis match that I think I should have won, I remind myself that in the bigger picture it doesn't matter. That's what a personal definition does for us. It makes it easier for us to see the bigger picture. It's a reference. It makes it easier to remember what's really important, and to realize that most of our worry points are just balloons full of air, just paper tigers.

Review your definition and evaluate it for its ability to claim a sense of purpose and power in your life right now. You can revisit your definition at any time you feel it's appropriate, including now if you wish. This is the whole point of this program: **You can redefine yourself whenever you wish.**

One of the most overlooked tools of development for the topic of questions is asking for help. Never underestimate your ability to get help from others in reaching your objectives. Obviously it helps if you can offer something in return for the help you are asking for. The simple fact that you are asking for help offers the person you're asking a chance to show their expertise and be of service. There is real value in this. You might be surprised by the help you are offered. Find someone who has accomplished what you hope to accomplish and ask their advice. The worst that can happen is they may refuse. And if you want someone's help, you should think of what you might do to help them.

The art of questions is an arena where we can learn a lot from children. They're full of questions. They're not shy about what they don't know. They're more interested in learning than in maintaining an image. Adults frequently don't ask questions because they are concerned about how they look. A question you need to keep asking is "What drives you?"

If we ask who do you want to be, we have another question we need to ask **We need to ask the question behind the question: Why are you here? Why are you here in this world?** Once we get past survival mode and providing ourselves with food, clothing, and shelter, we need to address this question and link the answer to the person we need to be. Without addressing the reason we're here, our design work won't have the necessary guiding light. We could work on designing our identity to be someone who might appear desirable, but we wouldn't have the five-star authenticity, the divine connection with the engine that drives us.

Most of us are struggling in one way or another. It's not because of what we don't have. It's because we're not lined up with who we are meant to be. We're out of sync. Every step that we take that is not in line with our natural purpose will encounter resistance. When we move into line with our natural purpose, there is no resistance. There will be obstacles and there will be work to be done, no doubt, but we will be going with the flow, moving in the direction intended for us.

Mother Teresa dedicated her life to working for the good of others. Martin Luther King Jr. dedicated himself to the establishment of civil rights. They certainly faced obstacles and worked hard for the causes that they dedicated themselves to, but they were clear about who they were and what they wanted. They didn't feel the internal resistance that most of us experience when we're not fully aligned with our purpose.

The fact is there's an abundance of evidence that there is a higher power at work in the universe. There is the sheer complexity of our mental and physical makeup and the laws of the universe. While it cannot be proven in a straightforward way, the belief in a higher power sets forth a powerful and purposeful way to look at the world. Whether it be Jesus Christ, Allah, the God of others, or a simple belief in an unnamed higher power, such beliefs provide shape for our sense of place and purpose. Conversely, when you think of it, if there is no God, no higher power, then life and everything that goes with it seemingly becomes a series of random events. This is not an empowering way to live. We can see that we have significance when we accept the fact that there is a higher power.

When it comes to recognizing our personal "profound significance," Les Parrott and Neil Clark Warren, both PhDs, psychologists, and authors of *Love the Life You Live*, suggest the two most obvious paths are to earn it or to recognize it. If you take the position that you have to earn it by doing something incredible, that leaves you vulnerable until such time as you accomplish something that meets your criteria. And you may never really feel satisfied despite a lifetime of hard work. It could be that as you reach one goal you form a new one, thus your effort to earn significance becomes a question of hitting a moving target.

The most direct path to acknowledging our personal significance in this world is simply to recognize it, to realize that God created you as a person of profound significance. In fact, this is the "only foundation for a truly healthy life." There is a God and He created you with purpose and significance. Once you recognize your own value, you can give value to others. Consequently, this leads to your understanding that whatever physical, emotional, or mental characteristics you have, you were endowed at birth with as much value as any person who will ever live. In other words, the phrase "All men are created equal" means exactly what it says, equal, not the same, but equal.

In accepting this fact, you assume a position of power in the universe. You've claimed your space on the world stage. The mere recognition of your place breeds a sense of confidence. If we are to design an identity of power, there can be no shortage of confidence. We can temper it with humility, but to be effective, we must move with confidence. And if any of this sounds a bit "grand" to you, you'd better get used to it. Designing personal power is a grand undertaking intended to deliver us from the day-to-day drift and grind.

So, when you ask "Do I matter?" the answer is, of course, you do. You need to come to the table with this belief because without it you'll have no reason to act with confidence and power. Without this core belief, anything written here or anything that could be written will have no foundation for power in your identity, and without this there is no path to the life you want.

Every choice we make from here on out, from the questions we ask to any answers we accept, the thoughts we think, and the actions we take, needs to be guided by the fact that we are designing for confidence and power. Not at the expense of others, but so we can be strong enough to live the life we want to benefit ourselves and others. A constant awareness question for everything we think and everything we do is simply "Where is this leading?" Where is this thought leading me? Where are these actions leading me? Are they leading me somewhere I want to be? Are they leading me somewhere I don't want to be? You can ask yourself this all day long.

For example, if you're targeting a slimmer, more vibrant body, you can ask this with every bite you eat. Is this leading me where I want to be? Is this efficient healthy fuel for my body? Or is this something I'm really better off without.

Questions for Winners

We've discussed some great questions that we can consider to drive us to focus our development and to serve as a springboard for our identity design work. Rather than simply think of these questions as you read this book, your design work will be better served if you can integrate these questions and their accompanying focus into your everyday life. We can do this by taking seven insistent questions, questions that push our growth buttons and ignite our daily transformation, and arranging them into a weekly schedule so we are always mindful of what we are doing, but more importantly, of who we are being!

Who am I now? Who am I going to be today?

While this is the core question, the core quest for identity design, there is a more specific way that we can use this question as part of our design project. The fact is we can choose to model ourselves after someone for any or many of the roles that we have. For example, at some time or another, we may need to be a peacemaker. Some individuals in our family, or at work, or at school, may be involved in some kind of dispute and you can see the problem it's causing them and others around them. You would like to help them resolve their differences. You would like to help them make peace. Is there a role model for you to follow? Who can you think of as a model person to guide you in this task? Think of a model for yourself. DO THIS NOW.

Whoever your model peacemaker may be, think of how she or he would address the situation and the individuals involved. Look for a way to apply these ideas to the task at hand. Someone who comes to mind for me is Nelson Mandela, a man who brought peace and freedom to South Africa, a man who said, "If you want to make peace with your enemy, you have to work with your enemy. Then he becomes your partner."

For another example, think of kids and sports. As kids play sports, they model the great athletes of their favorite sports. As a young hockey player in Detroit I idolized Gordie Howe, and "Gordie" became one of my nicknames. In backyard hockey games at my friend's house, I would announce my exploits as the great Red Wings forward. Mr. Fox would regularly tell me to pipe down so as not to annoy the neighbors, and after a brief period of compliance, I would get carried away again and draw a further warning. At the time, playing hockey was my favorite thing to do. Modeling Mr. Howe seemed completely natural. Watch kids play any sport anywhere in the world, and you'll find this ritualistic modeling at work. Here, as elsewhere, we can learn a lot from kids.

I have been using the modeling concept to help my tennis game. Great tennis players are constantly moving their feet when the ball is in play. A professional may take on average twice as many steps between shots as an amateur, and these additional steps ensure that the pro is always in the most optimum possible position to strike the ball. A player with less agile footwork will find themselves too close or too far to swing with maximum power in striking the ball. A good player is basically on the balls of their feet "dancing." I like to think of the great dancer Mikhail Baryshnikov and remind myself to keep moving, to keep dancing, when I play. When I serve, I think of the Marvel comic book hero the Mighty Thor, who fluidly swings his hammer and sends it hurtling at blinding speed toward his foes. Modeling as adults may take some additional thought, but it's a great way to adapt.

Here is a list of questions that you can cycle through on a weekly basis:

- What am I doing differently? How am I going to act differently?
- What am I going to improve? How have I improved?
- What have I let go? What am I going to let go of? (We could also ask, "How am I holding myself back?")
- What have I achieved? What am I achieving?
- What have I enjoyed? What am I enjoying?
- What did I make happen? What am I making happen?
- How have I served? How am I going to serve?

For our next activity, we can look at the question of freedom and how we perceive it. Are you free? Do you want to be free? Write out whether you believe you are free or not, and if so, what it means to be free, or if not, explain the ways that you are not free. DO THIS NOW.

Welcome back. Look at what you've written and think about how your responses to these questions affect your sense of personal power. People who acknowledge a high degree of satisfaction are those who feel they have a great deal of control over their lives. They control their destiny.

If someone doesn't believe they are free, they cannot feel that they are in control of their lives. Our sense of freedom and our sense of control go hand in hand. This concept of freedom and control is directly contrary to the concept that other people can "make you mad." This is another reason we need to recognize that when somebody does something and we get angry, we "choose" to get angry. **"Choose" is the operative word. No one "makes" us anything.** Our anger at some things that people do may well be justified, such as when we see someone take advantage of someone who is weaker or more vulnerable than them, but the fact remains that our anger is a choice.

When people ask me what I do and I tell them I'm a juvenile court judge in Detroit and that I hear cases of juvenile crime and parental neglect and abuse of children, the nearly universal response that I get is some variation on the following questions: "What?," "How do you manage to get through the day?," "Isn't that terribly depressing?" I can assure you these are not the questions I ask myself each day as I head in to work at the Lincoln Hall of Justice. While it's true I hear some horrific things from time to time, my focus is not on the question of how am I going to survive another horror story—and believe me I've heard my share, I've survived the photographs. I go to work each day with a different question: How can I help—how can I be of service? This is the kind of question that makes it a pleasure to do what I do.

Think of doctors in the emergency room. They too see horrific things, and I expect they look at things in a similar way. Patients arrive in extreme pain. The doctors see an opportunity to help someone get past the initial trauma stage and take their first steps toward recovery. While not everybody makes it, they have the satisfaction of knowing that however difficult their work is, they are on the front line of service to those in the greatest pain, and that's a beautiful place to be. Doctors, in general, are healers who help us all with every sort of physical ailment.

So, the question I ask as I go to work is a constant reminder of the first thing I love about my job. I get paid to help people. That's like hitting the lottery on a daily basis. I am reminded of when I wanted to play pro hockey and get paid for playing a game I loved. This is superior to that because I can provide more value. I have to confess that until I ran for election to serve as a judge, I was not nearly so well connected to the concept of a life of service.

I had a very challenging campaign, and I went virtually everywhere I could in Wayne County asking voters to give me their vote. As I did this, I became wedded to the idea that I wanted to serve and dedicated to the idea that if I was given a chance I would prove I was deserving by serving from the heart. And I can recall the thoughts I had in the last weeks before the election when I thought about the fact that I could win or I could lose. At the end of a long election night, I would simply be looking at a paper with two names, mine and my opponent's, with a number after each name reflecting the number of votes received. The course of my life was going to be determined by those two numbers. If the number after my name was greater, I would be elected judge, and if it was fewer, I would go back to what I was doing. And I didn't want to go back to what I was doing. I wanted to do more. I wanted to serve. And the people of Wayne County gave me that chance. I am thankful to this day.

The other thing I love about what I do is witnessing the change. When people realize that they need to change their approach to life, it's amazing to see the transformation that this brings. It's very common to see young people initially come to court under a dark cloud. Their life at home and in the community is full of chaos and challenges, and they come to court charged with an offense that reflects their low self-esteem, poor impulse control, a lack of discipline, and poor judgment. They've often been the victims of neglectful or abusive parenting, and they associate with individuals who are up to no good. Drug use is an issue most of the time as well.

After receiving services that include group and individual counseling and oftentimes a placement in a facility that works with juvenile offenders, individuals often show marked changes in behavior and attitude and essentially redefine themselves. We hold ninety-day periodic hearings to discuss progress and adjust services as needed. This is an opportunity to acknowledge the work that's been done, and in cases where progress is minimal, to explore the thoughts that are holding someone back. One of the most common themes of these discussions is the connection between actions and consequences. Actions have consequences. What kind of consequences can we expect from the actions we take? We have lives that show up based on the thoughts we have and the actions we take.

Who am I spending my time with? How are they influencing me? How am I influencing them? These are some things you can ask yourself on a daily or even hourly basis to be conscious of social influences. You can even start your day thinking of the people you will be interacting with during the course of the day, and thinking about how you would like these interactions to be. You won't be able to anticipate every person you will meet, but you can expect to interact with family members, coworkers, classmates, or friends. Most of your primary contacts can be anticipated, and you can decide how you will greet people and what quality of interaction you wish to have. This puts you in the driver's seat and sets you up to be proactive rather than reactive.

What if I told you there was a world where you wouldn't be judged by what you have, by the car that you drive, the phone that you carry, or the clothes that you wear?

What if I told you that in this world you wouldn't be judged by what you've done, by what failures or rejections you've experienced, or even by what successes you've had?

What if I told you that in this world you wouldn't be limited in any way by what others think of you?

What if I told you that you could choose to be whoever you wanted to be, that you were free? Who wants to be free? What if I told you this world exists and that it is at your command? In fact, it is. In fact, you are free.

We are not finished with questions in this program. In fact, we're just getting started. Questions can pull you forward or hold you back. Successful people know enough to ask empowering questions. It's their nature. Their identity leads them to ask empowering questions. So, start asking questions, and don't stop.

○⊂⊃ POINTS TO REMEMBER: ⊂⊃○

- If we are not happy most of the time, we either don't know who we are, or we know who we are but we are not being true to ourselves.
- When we define ourselves, we can begin to ask what's relevant to our lives.
- The Three Lies of Identity: You are what you have. You are what other people think of you. You are what you've done.
- We need to recognize that we are in the "choosing" business.
- We need to "choose" our identity, separate and apart from what we have, what others think of us, or what we've done.
- Our questions shape our internal conversation, and our conversation shapes our identity.
- We need to kill all the victim questions.
- What doesn't kill you makes you stronger.
- Create a one-sentence definition for yourself.
- You can redefine yourself whenever you wish.
- The question behind the question is: Why are you here?
- The most direct path to acknowledging our personal significance in this world is simply to recognize it.
- Our thoughts and actions need to be guided by the fact that we are designing for confidence and power.
- "Choose" is the operative word. No one "makes" us anything.

THE OWNERSHIP IDENTITY

A man can fail many times, but he isn't a failure
until he begins to blame someone else.
——John Burroughs

There are two primary choices in life: to accept conditions
as they exist, or accept the responsibility for changing them.
——Denis Waitley

The happiest people in the world are those who feel absolutely
terrific about themselves, and this is the natural outgrowth of
accepting total responsibility for every part of their life.
—Brian Tracy

Taking responsibility for being exactly where you are
gives you the power to be exactly where you want to be.
—Anonymous

Do you own your life? In order to get the life you want, you need to own your life. You need to adopt the ownership identity. This means you take responsibility for what shows up in your career, your relationships, your finances, and your life. All of it. When you realize that your life is yours to live and you are responsible, you exercise the power that every successful, productive person does. You can't afford the time to blame others because that simply gives them your power. You need it. Take control, take ownership.

Are you responsible? Do you see yourself as responsible for your life? What amount of control do you exercise over your day-to-day, moment-to-moment existence? If there's one principle you can expect to find in virtually every work on character development, it is the need to take responsibility. It's a constant whether it's expressed or implied. I have no intention of breaking from that pattern. And for those of us who believe that events are in God's hands or subject to the higher power of the universe, I do not see this as inconsistent with the need to accept responsibility. This is consistent with the statement that God helps those who help themselves. Fair enough. The ownership identity is also not about owning things. We've already discussed at length how damaging it can be to confuse who we are with what we have when we discussed the first big lie of identity. We are using the word ownership here as an expression of absolute responsibility.

You own the world. You own your world. Has anyone ever told you that? The fact is each of us has our own world in the sense that no two people have the same identical thoughts or outlook; no one has the same outlook as you do. Someone walks into a room to tell two people, Tom and Jennifer, that it's just started to rain. Tom is disappointed because he was planning to play tennis, and Jennifer is happy because her garden needs water—one event, two different responses based on two different outlooks. Something is always happening around us. Whatever it is, we don't want to be pushed or pulled out of character. Anger, frustration, or fear can all lead us to be off balance and to act in a way that is damaging or unproductive. We need to maintain our balance and our power.

There is a common expression that someone can "lose their grip." This expression is used to describe this very phenomenon. When someone loses their grip, they lose their power and they act out of vulnerability. Anger results in heated, irrational actions. Frustration leads us to be irritated, plagued, disturbed. These are not powerful states. Fear can be the most disabling of these states. We have the expression "frozen with fear," which pretty much says it all. We are not able to act with power when we are gripped by fear.

When we recognize the world as a place we own, we leverage all our abilities with confidence. **We can consciously choose to see the world as a place where events and circumstances are designed for our benefit.** Sometimes, this may seem to take the shape of an obstacle course we are required to run. Marines in basic training run obstacle courses to develop their ability to take on challenging conditions they may face on the battlefield. Our preparedness is as necessary as that of any marine. Claiming ownership sets us up with the frame of mind we need to access the life we want. Claiming ownership leads us to acknowledge that we have the energy we need to do what needs to be done.

If we intend to "be" in a dominant and fulfilling way, we need to adopt the ownership identity. **The ownership identity is somewhat self-explanatory in the sense that we take ownership for what comes to us—the good, the bad, and the ugly. It's ours. We recognize ourselves as a cause in the matter of what we experience in life.** This means we withdraw from the blame game and the pity party. There is no pity to be had, and we ask for none. To get the life we want we don't need pity, we need power. We need the power we inherently have. We no longer blame others or circumstances for our results. We embrace the fact that our results are just that, our results. If we want to blame someone else then we are actually surrendering our power to them. We are accepting the fact that they are responsible for the results in our lives and we are not. That is unacceptable to the ownership identity.

We want to own our experiences so we can exercise our control over them. Surveys indicate that a sense of control over one's life is the leading indicator of life satisfaction. There's a simple logic in this. After all, how can we expect to enjoy our life if we don't control it? The fact that we do control it, and we know we control it, makes all the difference.

We have all seen someone doing something improper, such as an aggressive driver cutting us off on the freeway. We respond with the thought that they've made us angry. This may seem natural, yet the fact is they didn't make you angry. They cut you off, and you chose anger as your response. When you take on the ownership identity, you understand that your response to any action is in your control and nobody else's. When someone cuts you off they've interrupted your driving pattern, but when you choose to get angry and stay angry for any length of time, you have given them the authority to interrupt your thought pattern. You allow someone in a car who you've never met, someone you never will meet, to dictate your thoughts when you focus your anger at them. And this happens anytime you get angry at anyone. Anger focuses your thoughts on something or someone in a nonproductive way. The fact is that unless you're getting everything done the way you want, anger is a luxury we cannot afford.

Let's look at some areas you may be challenged in through some statements that reflect the problem.

- I'm always late.
- I eat too much.
- I don't make enough money.
- I get angry all the time.

Select five areas that you are challenged in and write a statement that corresponds to each area, such as the statements above. DO THIS NOW.

Now, in a Jack Canfield exercise, we will exercise our ownership identity as it relates to these challenges. Look at the statements as written and rewrite each statement, but this time insert the word "choose" into the statement to acknowledge and declare your ownership of the corresponding challenge in your life. Thus, a statement such as "I eat too much" becomes "I choose to eat too much." DO THIS NOW.

Think about how different this statement feels now with this simple change. There's an undeniable ring of ownership in the statement now, and that's exactly what we are angling for with the concept of the ownership identity. Take a fifteen-minute period, and whatever you do during that fifteen minutes, think to yourself consciously, or even better, say aloud, "I choose to get up. I choose to go. I choose to call my brother, etc., etc., etc."

You'll find there's a different feel to what you're doing when you recognize consciously that you are choosing to do things rather than just doing them. Much of what we do is habit but we are still choosing. In the example above, we are still "choosing" to eat too much. You can repeat this activity daily for a week to develop and reinforce your sense of ownership. After that, to maintain contact with this concept, take one moment a day to focus on the fact that you are choosing to do whatever it is you are doing until you have fully ingrained this feeling and have made your ownership feeling second nature.

My son plays in the Eagle Sports church soccer league at Grace Community Church in Detroit. The league has three overriding rules that are taught as part of the culture of the league by the league founder, Terry Brennan. Players are taught: We never argue, we never complain, and we never make excuses. Why? Because we can't argue, complain, or make excuses and play soccer at the same time. The point is the kids are there to have fun and play soccer and that's what they do. Not a bad set of rules for life. How productive can you really be when you are engaged in any of these things? Arguing, complaining, and making excuses are not productive activities. They waste time and energy, and they disrupt focus. If you ask most people what they could really use to improve their lives, that's likely what most would tell you—more time, more energy, and more focus.

Make a list of things you have argued or complained about in the last week. Make a list of excuses you've made in the last week. If you want to be more inclusive, you can include things from the last month or year. DO THIS NOW.

Look over your list and consider how much time, energy, and focus you've lost as a result of what you see on your list. Above your list, write these words: I lose time, energy, and focus when I do the following. Think about adopting this set of rules as a way of maintaining your time, energy, and focus. And note how these rules are perfectly consistent with the ownership identity. **The ownership identity doesn't have time to argue, complain, or make excuses.**

Our nation was founded on the principle that all men are created equal. Can it be any other way? The fact is others may "have" more than you do. But does that make them any more important or any more valuable than you? How could it? Do you become more valuable on payday when you have more money? Of course not. You may "have" more, but your intrinsic value doesn't change.

We need to connect ourselves with the fact that our personal value is equal to that of any other person who walks the earth. If someone has more than we do then they can buy more than we can, but they can't "be" more than we can be. Buddha, one of the most influential persons who ever lived, wandered around the world teaching his philosophy. He inspired millions to follow his teachings of simplicity and peace. He didn't have possessions. What he did have was one of the most "centered"personalities, one of the strongest identities of all time. And he inspired millions to follow his teachings of simplicity and peace with the mere power of his identity and his intellect. The fact is the power of identity is worth more than gold.

One of the keys to the ownership identity is simply acceptance. We need to initially accept our circumstances for the moment even if we are hellbent on changing them because the fact is, if nothing else, our current circumstances are our starting point. This is where you are, no matter where you're headed, no matter where you want to go. Accepting this eliminates an additional source of resistance in your life. Of course, others may appear to be more fortunate than you, and others less fortunate. What's the point of focusing on this? Does it empower you in any way? How? This can remind us of the value of seeing life as designed for our benefit. **What if you simply adopted the thought that your life is perfect right now? Perfect for you. All your challenges at this moment—perfect.**

Earlier we discussed the benefits of believing in God or what some might refer to as a higher power in the universe. There are recent efforts to evaluate the benefits of spiritual beliefs. Over 300 carefully designed research studies indicate that people who are spiritually actualized live longer, have less stress, require less medication, and develop significantly fewer emotional and physical problems.

Take, for example, the study of Dr. Warren Berland who studied the amazing survival of thirty-three men and women diagnosed with cancer and given less than a 20 percent chance of surviving five years. Twenty-eight of the thirty-three had already lived more than five years, some as long as fifteen years, and the other five who had been given a more recent diagnosis were still alive, though none of their doctors expected them to be. Dr. Berland asked the patients themselves why they thought they were still alive, defying all odds. The single reason given by most patients was God. They simply believed God was more responsible for their survival than modern medicine. And these were individuals selected not because of their religious orientation, but because of their unexpected state of survival.

In a Duke University study, postoperative patients who engaged in spiritual practices averaged eleven days in the hospital while nonreligious patients averaged twenty-five days. A review of four major epidemiological studies (of 126,000 participants) concluded that "those frequently attending religious services had approximately 29 percent fewer deaths from all causes (over a specified time period) when compared with those who were not religiously active." A 1996 review of several studies indicated that spiritual practices and beliefs led to less alcohol and drug abuse, lower suicide rates, reduced criminal behavior, and higher marital satisfaction. **Believing has benefits.**

Taking ownership over our lives requires taking ownership of our decisions, our choices. Brain function research is shining a light on the factors and the process of decision making. We can use this information to help us understand what we do and why we do it. This, in turn, can help us reset our course and redesign our identity.

We could choose to simply blame circumstances or blame others for the results we see in our lives, but what does this get us? The fact is we start assessing blame at an early age, often to avoid parental discipline, and if we're not careful, this crutch can handcuff our development for the rest of our lives. It might appear to be a way to preserve our self-esteem but it actually does the opposite. Blaming others is a poor strategy. It destroys relationships. It prevents growth and fosters complacency.

In a recent article, "Why You Should Take the Blame," Peter Bregman, a strategic executive advisor, succinctly states his prescription: **Take the blame for anything you're even remotely responsible for.** This "solution" flips the switch, turning negatives to positives and, rather than surrendering power, you actually claim it. Taking responsibility liberates you. It reinforces your relationships and your credibility. You become easier to approach and your stance encourages constructive criticism that you might otherwise never hear. Taking the blame, as Bregman points out, is the power move because once you've taken responsibility for something, you can do something about it.

It takes courage to shoulder blame. It's proactive. And this places you in a leadership position. Think of the times a dominant player on a losing team, even when he or she has played well, will say, "I didn't do enough for us to win." In a team sport, no one person is ever solely responsible for a result, but the fact is when each player states that they didn't do enough, they acknowledge their power to impact the outcome, to create a result. This expression has been used so often I find myself saying, "Where have I heard that before?" each time I hear it.

In January 2014, two of the NFL's legendary quarterbacks squared off for the umpteenth time. In the AFC Championship Game to decide who would represent the conference in the Super Bowl, Peyton Manning and the Denver Broncos defeated Tom Brady and the New England Patriots. After the game, Tom Brady, who has won the Super Bowl three times, came out and acknowledged he didn't do enough for his team to win. If it's difficult for you to accept blame, you probably see it as a sign of weakness. Look at it as a sign of strength, an acknowledgement of power. Things that you can accept blame for are things you can cure the next time around. When the blame is up for grabs, grab it.

Another benefit of taking the blame is that it means there's no reason for anyone else to blame you. What's the point if you've already taken the blame? In a single stroke, you've put an end to the "blame you" conversation—that is, as long as you're sincere. If you're not, your insincerity only mocks others and creates more dissension. And after all, blame is really another word for responsibility. It has a negative connotation because it's used when things go wrong, but its underlying meaning is responsibility. Responsibility and control go hand in hand. If you want to feel in control, you've got to take responsibility. As you take responsibility, you naturally feel the control that follows from doing so. Think of your most important activities and the control you exercise regarding these activities.

In the book *Super Joy*, Paul Pearsall suggests an informative activity he uses in his counseling practice to address the issue of control and priorities. First, you need to list the activities or elements of life that you consider most important. Second, across from each activity or element, list the major block that you have that prevents you from making more of a commitment to these items. For example, if you consider exercise to be important and would like to have time to work out in the morning before work but are unable to do so because you stay up too late watching television, you could list exercise in your first column and across from it you could list watching TV. So, take a moment now and list five or more things you'd like to do more of and across from each list write down what is blocking you from giving more time to these things. DO THIS NOW.

Once you've done this take a look at your list and insert the word "or" between the two columns. You now have memorialized in writing the choices you are faced with regarding these important activities. This connects you to these choices and their consequences. The value of drawing up a list like this is to make you aware of the choices you are making "unconsciously." It lays out in simple terms what needs to change if you're going to spend more time on what you consider to be important. You can visualize a control panel with two rows of switches or buttons for these competing activities. Do you push the button in the "important" column or in the "blocking" column? The choice is yours. The control is yours. You just need to exercise it. Think of how efficient we can be by simply going through our day and flipping the right switches.

Philosopher analysts from Plato forward have theorized that the mind has two competing forces: the rational mind, which carefully weighs options and makes logical decisions based on this process, and the emotional mind, which acts on instinct and basic primal drives. In order to be effective, Plato argued the mind had to restrain emotional impulsive drives from interfering with rational thought. While our knowledge of the mind is still developing, science shows that things are much more complicated than that, and that emotions are a very significant and positive part of good decision making.

Evolution has led to the development of increasingly complex and specialized brains in the animal kingdom; however, until Homo sapiens appeared, all of these species lacked the ability to reflect on their decisions and to develop plans or language to express their inner thoughts. Until humans arrived, what couldn't be done automatically couldn't be done at all. We have these abilities, but it is how we use them that is critical. We can use them in a way that is harmful or helpful. We can drown ourselves in worry or look for joy in who we are and what we do. There are a million ways to look at things and no one looks at things exactly the way you do because no one has the same experience, the same background, the same character.

Self-improvement is a critical part of life but we need to start with self-acceptance. **The fact is self-acceptance is more important than self-improvement.** Without self-acceptance, you have no foundation to build from. The most you can do is improve something that you don't accept. Acceptance is an affirmation. Acceptance gives us a foundation for meaningful improvement. And this is a central pillar to the ownership identity.

The Acceptance Letter

Our next activity is to write an acceptance letter. This is probably unlike any acceptance letter you've ever read or written. You will be accepting yourself. Imagine you have applied for enrollment at a particular college, or applied for a position at a company, or auditioned for a role in a feature film. More than that, imagine you have applied for a position in the game of life. You've asked to be given the life of your dreams. Imagine that you've been accepted. Write the acceptance letter you've received. This is not a one-line statement of acceptance. Rather, this is a letter that outlines your unique characteristics that qualify you for this role. You can mention strengths as well as challenges. Your letter should acknowledge acceptance of the way you look, the way you feel, and the way you think as you are now.

If you're overweight and you want to change that, you can. But at this stage, you are setting a foundation by accepting yourself as you are now. You are accepting who you are and your responsibility for who you are. If you've eaten too much of the wrong food, you can take responsibility for this. If your relationships are fractured and troubled, accept it. All you're doing is realistically assessing where you're at and accepting it so you can acknowledge the power you've exercised in creating the life you have so far. And if you've had a bad break such as being injured in an auto accident through no fault of your own, acknowledge that you're a survivor.

Your letter should establish why you are perfect for this life and this life is perfect for you. Some of us have never really accepted ourselves. We continually beat ourselves up over all kinds of things, such as not having this, or not knowing that, or not being able to do this or that. If we are going to prosper, we need to start by accepting who we are, by acknowledging that we have been designed for a purpose. Write your letter. DO THIS NOW.

Another step we can take in establishing our ownership identity is to announce our plans and the goals we've set to friends, family, and colleagues. This is a form of commitment that makes it less likely that we will give up. In addition, this can build a support system for you to achieve your goals, although it's also possible that some may attempt to discourage you. Research has shown that people who announce their plans to others are more likely to follow through and be successful than those who keep their plans to themselves, as discussed in the book *59 Seconds: Think a Little, Change a Lot* by Richard Wiseman.

Now we have an activity to build the ownership identity within us. Take the next twenty-four hours and dedicate it to the power of choice. You can set your alarm again for half-hour intervals for your waking moments; each half-hour, as you check in, you simply recognize that whatever is going on with you is your choice.

Whatever you're feeling, whatever you're thinking, and whatever you're doing, it is your choice. You say to yourself, "I'm choosing to feel stressed, or productive, or happy, or sad. I'm choosing to work or play. I'm choosing to think about work, or the game, or my friend." You might think to yourself, *Well, I have to go to work.* Going to work is a choice. You need to own that this is your choice. You may not have the job that you want, which would not be unusual, but if that's the case then that should lead you to ask the question we talked about earlier: What am I going to do about it?

Recognizing choices that we make and that everything we do is a choice builds awareness that we are in control. We can represent this with an equation:

A + C = P or Awareness plus Choice equals Power.

Power is what we're after, NOT to dominate others but to assert ourselves in this world, to be willful in our lives. We're looking for progress here, and we can start with self-assessment with this power rating system. We can rate our overall effectiveness on a scale of one to ten on a daily basis and chart our progress. For example, let's say you have an issue in your relationship with a close friend or relative. Perhaps they have a habit of taking advantage of your good nature and are repeatedly asking for favors that are never returned. You see this person and again they ask you to run an errand or ask for some other favor. Do you accept the task without complaint as you have in the past or do you point out the imbalance in the relationship and press the issue?

The first response would be rated low on the power scale from zero to two, while the second response would be rated as an eight to ten, depending on how well it was handled. Once you get in the habit of rating yourself on a daily basis, you can begin to see an impact. There is an expression in the business field that "what gets measured, gets managed," and here as you measure your power, you manage your power.

One of the most powerful things we can do to build our ownership identity is to own our relationships and to take responsibility for our relationships with others. When it comes to relationships, we have to start with the question of who we are going to build and maintain relationships with. Careful attention to this question alone will reap major dividends for us in our lives. It's axiomatic that you are influenced by the people you associate with.

We are social beings. We were meant to connect with others. The quality of our lives is reflected in who we connect with and how we connect. Some people have a way of energizing us with their natural joy and self-assurance. Others are just difficult to be around. They always seem to be mad at something or someone. They have a negative compass. Have you ever thought to measure who's pulling you up and who's pushing you down? A friend of mine once told me he rated those of us he came into regular contact with over a thirty-day span. He rated each contact on a scale from one to ten as to whether the person appeared to be up, down, or just so-so on a given day. Then, he averaged out the ratings over the thirty days. His ratings were geared to measure the mood of his contacts, but this is only part of the equation. The more important question is not how these individuals feel, but how they influence you.

List at least five of your primary "contacts," which can include family, friends, work colleagues, etc. On a scale of one to ten, after each name, rate how you generally feel after contact with these individuals. Do they make you laugh or cry? Do they encourage you, or compliment you, or belittle you? Do they listen to you and talk to you, or do they seem only interested in themselves and do they talk "at" you? Do you generally feel relaxed or "on guard" around them?

These are just some of the questions you can ask to help you evaluate your contacts. You should feel free to add to these questions to enable you to consider anything that's relevant. Think of at least five contacts and go to work. You be the judge. DO THIS NOW.

Once you've done this, you can think about who you need to spend more time with and who you need less time with. For any of these individuals, regardless of where they fall on your scale, you can ask yourself what you can do to improve your relationship and the nature of your contacts with them. For any good relationship to flourish, you need two things: care and communication. You need to care about the person, to care about the relationship, and you need to communicate effectively. When I hold review hearings in juvenile court, I am working to establish and maintain a relationship with the young people and the parents whose cases are before me. The first task is to let them know that I care. I care about them and I care about their success.

I have made it a point to visit a number of the residential facilities where our young people are treated. One of these placements, Starr Commonwealth, is located in western Michigan. This is a nonsecure placement set on a beautiful rural campus. There are woods and ponds. I was there visiting on a beautiful summer day. Mark Bonello, one of the counselors who regularly appeared in my court, gave me a tour. As we were walking through the woods with the sunlight coming through the trees, he told me about discussions he had with some of the residents he counseled about their appearances in my court.

He said they were programmed, or geared, to look at law enforcement personnel, including judges, as the enemy. When they came to court and found themselves treated with care and respect and a genuine level of concern, it was a game changer in the sense that it pushed them to look at the law enforcement "system" in a new way. They opened up to the concept that this was not simply a system designed to punish them for whatever they did wrong, but that there was a genuine effort being made to help them develop their lives in a positive way. I've never forgotten this conversation, and I've redoubled my efforts to communicate my concern to the young people who appear before me. As my friends on the Youth Deterrent Team like to say, "They don't care what you know until they know that you care."

I take the same approach with parents in my court, especially those who get entangled in abusive relationships. It's sad to see people endure these relationships, which sometimes include life-threatening beatings. These relationships aren't built on appreciation, but on manipulation. Only a severe identity crisis can allow this to happen.

In a healthy relationship, when you care about someone, you are willing to be giving to that person, and you can do that every time you talk to them. In today's world of nonstop interruptions, the art of listening is more valuable than ever. True listening means being fully present with someone when you talk with them. This means you stop checking your phone or computer and listen. An especially good technique to assure good communication is to repeat back points that your friend makes to you. **Develop your ability to listen, to relate, and to understand by using "What you're saying is . . ." statements.** When you repeat something back to your friend, you support them by showing you're truly listening, and you confirm that you understood what they intended to tell you. Work on this over the next week. At least twice a day when you are in a conversation, respond by repeating a point your friend makes.

The gold standard in owning relationships is something I learned when I participated in a seminar called the Landmark Forum. This is an unusual seminar in which one hundred or more people gather in a room for discussions about life. The sessions are guided by experienced forum leaders. The discussions reminded me of the kinds of things you talk about with your college roommates late at night in those moments when you are feeling your way through what life is, how it works, and what really matters, like the classic college bull session. An essential part of the forum is the creation of a sense of community among the attendees and the forum leader. I participated in the forum weekend and a follow-up event referred to as the advanced course. There was an in-depth discussion about how we manage our relationships and how we respond to conflict. The Landmark approach to maintaining positive relationships is to look for the fix and not the fault.

When we are committed to a relationship with someone, and something we do or say upsets that person, a standard response is to fault them for getting upset. We tend to think they're being unreasonable because we don't think we've said or done anything to justify their response. Then, our response to their response is cold, given that we believe that they are wrong to be upset with us.

For example, let's say your wife expects you to make sure there is enough gas in the car so that she won't have to stop for gas in the early morning before taking your daughter to school. You forget to fill up and she is upset, given that the same thing happened before. You were distracted on the way home as a result of a major issue at work and you forgot. She is upset that you were thoughtless and careless about her request. You don't think she is justified to be as upset as she is. In this scenario, there's a certain amount of friction created that pushes both of you to be unhappy with each other. One response is that you can say it's her problem and she'll just have to get over it.

At Landmark, an alternative response was suggested for circumstances such as this. The fact is it's your relationship and you did something, or in this case failed to do something, that created a problem with your relationship. If you respond by simply saying it's her problem, you get the benefit of being able to claim to yourself that you're "right," but this does nothing to help you repair the relationship. We are attached to the concept of fault. Whenever a problem arises, our first reaction is to ask whose fault it is. Then, once we assign fault, the responsibility for fixing the problem follows the person we have blamed for the problem. **When you have a conflict in your relationship, look for the fix, not the fault.**

By blaming your wife, you shift the responsibility to her and surrender your power to repair the relationship. This is such a critical point that I need to repeat it for emphasis. When you blame someone else and assign the responsibility to them, you surrender the power to fix the problem. The alternative is to claim full ownership of the relationship and accept that it's your relationship and you did something to cause the problem, and given that you caused the problem, it is now within your power to fix it. This is referred to in the terminology of the Landmark Forum as acknowledging that you are a "cause in the matter." And this is really another way of saying, "I'm responsible for what shows up in my life," which is the central concept of the ownership identity.

The broader you apply this concept, meaning the more things that you consider yourself to be the cause of, the more power you claim in your life. Again, the concept is that, by definition, ownership is power. So once you accept that you have caused the problem, it's your responsibility to fix the problem. During the first year of my marriage to my wonderful wife, Viktoriya, we had many conflicts over various things, and it seems most of them were due to a misunderstanding of one kind or another. I remember thinking on many occasions that I was being tested. My first reaction was to think, "She's just not being reasonable here." The fact is I often didn't really know that what I'd said or done had been misinterpreted by her in the first place. English was not her first language, and the language barrier was sometimes the very source of the misunderstanding.

I remember thinking on these occasions about what we discussed at Landmark. This is my relationship. If there's a problem, then I must have done something to create it. If I created it, then I *can* do something to fix the problem. I *need* to do something to fix the problem. I *will* do something to fix the problem. As a result of these thoughts, my sense of ownership regarding the relationship would kick in, and I would work to repair the relationship with an apology and/or whatever other discussion or initiative I thought was necessary. I released the need to hold on to any claim that I was "right" and she was "wrong." This approach was invaluable in building the relationship I have with Viktoriya.

In fact, this highlights another Landmark lesson: **Any statement, by any person, at any time, can be interpreted by any other person in any way they choose.** Our lives are chock-full of misunderstanding. Statements and actions that are done with one purpose are so often interpreted by others in a very different way. A parent spanks his child thinking, "I love my son and I hate to do this, but my son has misbehaved, and if I don't spank him, he'll continue to misbehave and will grow up without any sense of discipline." The child who is spanked thinks, "My father is hitting me, he doesn't love me, and I'm a bad person."

This is why communication is so critical. Steven Covey, in his groundbreaking work, *The 7 Habits of Highly Effective People*, states the need "first to seek to understand, and then to be understood." The quality of your relationships and your life is governed by the quality of your communication. We all know it's important to listen and we need to listen to understand. We can develop this skill the same way we can take on any skill—with practice. For the next week, twice a day during conversations, in your own words repeat back to whomever you are speaking with something that they've said. Then, ask them to confirm that you have understood them properly. An example of this conversation could be as follows:

Tom—"I have a hard time understanding why it's so difficult to get some reasonable restrictions on guns in this country. Other countries, like Australia, that have restrictions don't experience these periodic shooting sprees that result in so many people being killed and injured. Years ago they had one of these horrible incidents, and they responded by passing laws that restricted firearms and, since then, they haven't had another one of these large-scale shooting sprees. Even if we retain the right for individuals to have guns, I don't see why people need to have these assault rifles that can kill fifteen people in an instant."

April—"Are you saying that with our experience here in the US, with shooting sprees on college campuses, high schools, and grade schools, resulting in multiple killings, we should have seen some gun restrictions passed into law by now to address the situation?"

Tom—"Yes, that's exactly what I'm saying!"

As we can see, April built on Tom's original comment with a specific reference to other incidents that are examples of what Tom was referring to. Listen first to understand, then to be understood. In the example above, Tom knows from April's responsive question that she understood his point. And April knows from Tom's confirmation that she understood. This is something you can do to reinforce your listening skills and to let others know that you really are listening. There's quite a difference demonstrating comprehension by restating what someone says in your own words as opposed to simply muttering, "Uh, yeah." So, practice this and see how it affects the quality of your conversation with others.

To take ownership of our relationships, we can get help in gaining perspective by asking others how we're doing. In an effort to do just that, I sent the following note via email to a small circle of friends and family:

Dear (the names have been omitted to protect the innocent):

Congratulations! You've been selected. I trust your ability to provide constructive criticism, and I'm hoping you'll participate in my constructive criticism survey. It's my hope to learn from this and to be able to take what I learn to improve my relationship with others as well as my character in general. A few questions follow, and I ask that you offer your assistance in the spirit with which I'm asking for it. This is a growth experiment.

What do you consider to be my strengths?

What do you consider to be my strengths in relating to others?

What do you consider to be my weaknesses?

What do you consider to be my weaknesses in relating to others?

Is there anything that you've observed, or anything you know of that I've done or failed to do, that was harmful to you or others? (Let me apologize in advance. Feel free to make this list as long as it needs to be, and to supply any details that will help me understand the impact of my actions.)

Can you suggest one area in which I could most improve?

Responses I received from these "survey letters" alerted me to blind spots, giving me insights into some things I really hadn't thought about. The responses were straightforward and fair and included some constructive criticism. Of course, this type of letter is asking for criticism, and if you are more interested in developing your character than hanging on to some notion that you're already one of the most wonderful people in the world, then this is a great way to get some insight from those that know you best.

When it is necessary to criticize anything someone has done, it's important to start with a positive comment and to be clear that you're criticizing only what they've done. You are criticizing their behavior. You are not attacking them personally. In court, I have these discussions with kids and their parents virtually every day. My goal is always to engage in a discussion as opposed to "lecturing" people. I realize that the black robe I wear doesn't come with any "magical" powers, and the formality of the courtroom doesn't change the basic rule that **you can influence people to change, but they are the only ones who can change themselves.** Without their personal commitment to change, your intention to change anyone is meaningless.

If I can engage someone, if I can get them to talk "to" me, I have a chance of influencing them. I work to persuade them that they should change. If they are only willing to comply with a court order because I have the power to penalize them if they don't comply, then they are only temporarily pushed into compliance while the court has jurisdiction in their case. They haven't actually changed.

Children can be particularly sensitive to criticism. Even when your words only criticize their behavior, they can take it as a complete assault on their self-image. Thus, it becomes especially important to make this clear. In talking to your children you can simply say, "I love you, but this is not acceptable behavior."

There's a lot to take ownership of in our lives, and it's the powerful way to be. Just as we equate control with power, ownership underlies control. So, now we should be ready to shoulder the blame, claim ownership, and seize the day.

As part of our 7/60 Mad Minute Identity Design Plan, we can dedicate a day to claiming the ownership of our lives. My schedule sets it for Thursday, but you can choose any day you like. On Thursday, ownership day, for one minute in the morning and one minute in the afternoon, focus on ownership. You are focusing on owning the results that are showing up in your life, not necessarily the possessions that you actually own. But if you've worked to earn the income to buy something you value, then you can focus on having created that result for yourself. But, beyond that, there's a wealth of other things to consider, such as your relationships. Think about owning the way the important people in your life respond to you. If their response is not what you would like it to be, consider what you will do to change it.

Resist the impulse to blame people or circumstances for the results you experience. Recognize that blaming others gives them a power over your life that should be yours. Ownership is about taking responsibility. As this sense of ownership becomes part of your identity, your sense of power will grow exponentially. You'll be right where you need to be in order to get the life you want.

oⵒ POINTS TO REMEMBER: ⵒo

- You own the world.
- We can consciously choose to see the world as a place where events and circumstances are designed for our benefit.
- The ownership identity is somewhat self-explanatory in the sense that we take ownership for what comes to us, the good, the bad, and the ugly. It's ours. We recognize ourselves as a cause in the matter of what we experience in life.
- The ownership identity doesn't have time to argue, complain, or make excuses.
- What if you simply adopted the thought that your life is perfect right now? Perfect for you. All your challenges at this moment—perfect.
- Believing has benefits.
- Take the blame for anything you're even remotely responsible for.
- The fact is self-acceptance is more important than self-improvement.
- A + C = P or Awareness plus Choice equals Power.
- One of the most powerful things we can do to build our ownership identity is to own our relationships.
- Develop your ability to listen, to relate, and to understand by using "What you're saying is . . ." statements.
- When you have a conflict in your relationship, look for the fix, not the fault.
- Any statement, by any person, at any time, can be interpreted by any other person in any way they choose.
- You can influence people to change, but they are the only ones who can change themselves.

THE CHALLENGE IDENTITY

There are no negatives in life, only challenges to overcome that will make you stronger.
—Eric Bates

If you aren't in over your head, how do you know how tall you are?
—T.S. Eliot

You will face your greatest opposition when you are closest to your biggest miracle.
—Shannon L. Alder

It's not enough that we do our best; sometimes we have to do what's required.
—Winston Churchill

Challenges in life can either enrich you or poison you. You are the one who decides.
—Steve Maraboli

If it doesn't challenge you it doesn't change you.
—Fred DeVito

Expect problems and eat them for breakfast.
—Alfred A. Montapert

I dentity design for the life we want requires a powerful mindset to address any obstacles we face. Even when things are going well, we face challenges. When things are not going well, sometimes it seems our lives are nothing but a dense and imposing forest of obstacles. Perhaps you can think of some times when you felt overrun by challenges, when you gave up on some task or goal, or you nearly gave up as a result. Adopting a confident and assertive approach to challenges is absolutely critical. Without it, we are sure to encounter roadblocks that can prevent us from driving through to our destination. It is time for us to examine our attitude toward challenges of all kinds and to shift into power mode.

Think about the expression, "What doesn't kill you makes you stronger." Can you see how this expression can be applied to your experiences? Think of an obstacle you've faced. It may be something you failed to conquer, or it may be something that was extremely difficult but that you eventually overcame. In either case, it should be something that you can recall you wish you didn't have to deal with at the time. Think of something that tried your patience. Maybe you had an accident, or had a setback at work or school, or just had a big task or challenge you had to take on.

Take this experience and imagine for a moment that you are the higher power of the universe. Consider that, as the higher power, you determined that this experience that you are recalling is something that you designed specifically as a "growth experience" for yourself. Picture yourself as the prime mover of the universe, carefully crafting this challenge for no other purpose than to spur your development. DO THIS NOW.

In fact, isn't this what actually happened? **Didn't the universe challenge you so you could grow stronger?** Didn't the universe give you this experience so you could grow stronger in responding to it?

Let me share a personal example from my campaign to be elected judge. When I decided to run for a seat that was being vacated by a retiring judge, I put the word out early that I planned to run and hoped that my candidacy might dissuade others from choosing to run. I was almost successful, almost. There just happened to be an individual from a family with the most recognizable name in Wayne County judicial politics who was also interested in running for this particular seat. In the interest of saving myself the challenge of having to run a campaign against this formidable opponent, I invited him to lunch and proposed that he choose another open seat to run for, and I suggested he would have a greater chance of success in this other race. Well, as luck would have it, my plea fell on deaf ears. He was interested in the seat I had chosen to run for, and that's all there was to it.

In an instant, I went from receiving a free pass by having no opposition to facing the most formidable campaign challenge I could think of. Ah, the joy of a challenge. While I cannot say I was infused with joy at the time, I had made my choice and he had made his and the race was on. This campaign clearly rates as one of the single greatest growth experiences of my life. A yearlong campaign in a vast and diverse county of almost two million people required numerous personal appearances and presentations, a great amount of team building, and a lot of coordination of services of all of those who were kind enough to help me. When I look back on it now, I am grateful to my opponent, Dan Hathaway, for the challenge he provided and for what was required of me. And I consider this to be a perfect example of a challenge I was given that spurred my personal growth. (Dan was elected two years later with the highest vote total of all the candidates in a race for three open circuit court seats.)

So if that's the case, if we can begin to look at all of our obstacles this way, we can make a fundamental change in our response pattern. Life is a perception game. **We construct our reality as we perceive it.** The key to our effectiveness and our joy is to manage our perceptions and responses. We don't control the events, we control our response to the events, and the key to our response is our perception . . . our perception and our identity. And our identity affects our perception, which is another reason why our identity is so important. It frames the way we see the world. This determines our response pattern. Think of it this way:

$$\frac{\textbf{Event}}{\textbf{Perception}} = \textbf{Input} + \textbf{Identity} = \textbf{Response}$$

There is a thread of thought that states that everything in the universe is perfect as it is. You are your perfect self and every event in your life is designed perfectly for your absolute growth and development. This is discussed by Chris Prentiss in his book *Be Who You Want, Have What You Want.* Whether you agree with this, I think you would have to admit that this can be a very empowering way to look at your world and your place in it. But, of course, you might say what about war, what about torture, what about the bad things that happen to innocent children, there's nothing perfect about that. Let me be frank . . . I don't have the answer for this. If I did, I would be running the universe, offering unconditional love to all. I would be God.

There are mysteries that you and I will never know in this lifetime. Yet our objective is to take what we do know and build the life we want. To do this, we need to find ways to look at the world that reinforce our sense of power. There is no way that we can achieve the life we want unless we find a powerful way of being.

Thinking that the world is designed for our benefit is a powerful way to be. It tells us that obstacles and hurdles that we face are not rocks to grind us down but trampolines designed to help us jump to the next level. They are uniquely designed by the highest power in the universe for our continual growth and development. We grow in this world or we die. If we are not progressing, we are going nowhere, and if we're going nowhere, we might as well be dead.

What am I suggesting when I ask you to consider adopting a viewpoint like this? Look, you have a choice to make as to how you view the world. That view is central to your identity. It's up to us to find the view that resonates within us and drives us to be effective and powerful. When we learn something new, we can supplement our world view or substitute it altogether. If we want to grow and develop, we have to have beliefs that say "Now you have this in your life, and this is going to move you forward." It's only a matter of how far and how fast.

Carol Dweck, the Lewis and Virginia Eaton Professor of Psychology at Stanford University, has extensively researched the topic of mindset in students and athletes. She identifies two mindsets people hold about ability. Some people maintain a fixed mindset, one that sees talents as gifts. For these individuals, they have what they have, and they perceive their level of success as a reflection of the talent they possess. Others maintain a growth mindset. They believe that their abilities can be developed by effort and practice. They recognize that some individuals are better than others at certain tasks, but they believe that everyone can improve with practice. Any natural ability or lack of ability that a person has is not a limit; it's merely a starting point.

You might think that it's more important to simply have confidence in your native ability to be successful, but research on this topic indicates that this can actually serve as a liability in the hands of an individual with a fixed mindset. For individuals who see themselves as capable based on their talent, they see tasks not as opportunities to learn and grow but as challenges to their self-image. Any setback they experience can serve as a blow to their self-concept. Thus, they can choose to avoid anything too challenging that might make them look like a "failure." They seek out only activities at which they can expect to excel.

It's like the tennis player who avoids practicing their backhand because it's the weak part of their game, or the basketball player who practices the one shot that he's good at to the exclusion of all others. It's great to have certain strengths to rely on, but we can't expect to grow and improve unless we step out of our comfort zone.

Dweck describes these individuals as concerned with "performance goals" as opposed to "learning goals," which are the goals of individuals who are willing to risk failure in order to grow, to improve, and to learn. **Her research shows that when you praise students for their intelligence rather than their effort, they actually become less motivated.** This sets them up to be more concerned about performance than learning, which leads to the "protectionism" described above. **Praising intelligence praises what is, while praising effort praises the process of what one is becoming. We need a growth mindset.** (Marina Krakovsky. "The Effort Effect." *Stanford Magazine* March/April 2007. Electronic.)

The motto here is "Better to grow than to stick with what you know." This is the challenge process. That old cliché about challenges being opportunities gets repeated for a reason. It's a golden rule in the field of identity design. **You want more power? Start looking for challenges.** Start looking at challenges as your best chance to learn and grow.

In fact, we can all accept an overall challenge of constant advancement, constantly improving ourselves. What parts of your life and what activities are you involved in at this time that involve personal growth or learning? If nothing comes to mind, you need to add something to the mix. Why shouldn't we be more each day? The status quo isn't any place to live. The brain isn't meant to be a static organ.

Its design is uniquely geared to thrive on continual development. Neuroscientific research now indicates that experience can cause changes in the brain's physical structure and functional organization.

The whole thrust of identity design is to spur an ongoing development of powerful neural pathways to support a dynamic way of being. Once this is established as an integral part of who you are, the heavy lifting is done. You become so connected to your growth identity that the thought of "coasting" without growth becomes repulsive. Instead, you can look to learn the way a child does.

Think of the child's approach. When faced with something new, a child delights in exploring and discovering whatever he or she can. There is no fear that this exploration might expose the child's lack of knowledge or embarrass the child in some way because, frankly, those are grownup concepts that a child has to learn before they become meaningful, before they start tying us down and holding us back. Unfortunately, many grownup concepts are counterproductive. When it comes to opportunities to learn, it's better to be the child. When we're not engaged in some form of development, we stagnate and find ourselves caught within the web of what we know: the "comfort zone."

Now, let's take on another daily awareness activity. Spend a day in which you check in with yourself throughout the day with this thought: I am living in a perfect world in which every event is designed for my benefit. Every event is designed for my benefit. The challenge here is to adopt this mindset and to experience the liberation that comes from seeing things this way. Rather than life being a series of hardships, you see events and your experiences as building blocks for the platform of your ultimate development.

One key to our attitude toward challenges is our use of metaphors. A metaphor is a figure of speech in which a word or phrase literally denoting one kind of object or idea is used in place of another to suggest a likeness or analogy between them (such as "drowning in money"). We hear metaphors all the time and many of us use them without realizing it. **Metaphors are powerful indicators of our attitudes.** Have you heard the expression, "It's a dog eat dog world"? Is this how you or someone you know looks at the world? Well, if you do, it says that we're all dogs, and we're either dogs that are being eaten by other dogs, or we are dogs that are eating other dogs. Does this sound like a healthy way to look at the world?

Metaphors are powerful figures of speech because they reflect and enhance understanding through the connection of two distinct and separate concepts, creating a hybrid image. The formation of a metaphor is itself a creative act of fusion. And the power of the image created can be very positive or very negative. I've employed a number of metaphors in this book. The train imaginization activity is built on the metaphoric vision of a train dumping negative experiences. The do-it-now muscle, the now wheel, the foundational wall, the giving tree, and the symphony of life, are all metaphors.

Some writers, such as Anthony Robbins, have suggested the quality of our lives can be measured in the quality of our metaphors. The fact is the metaphors we use reflect our attitudes in a unique way. They generally link the way that we think to an image of some kind, and since a picture is "worth a thousand words," **metaphors pack a powerful punch in the world of self-talk.**

A related figure of speech is the simile. A simile is a figure of speech that compares two things using words such as "like" or "as" or, in the case of verbs, the word "than." Let's look at some common metaphors and similes.

- What matters isn't the size of the dog in the fight—it's the size of the fight in the dog.
- Problems are like hills: They look hopelessly steep from a distance, but when we approach them, they flatten out.
- It is better to wear out than to rust out.
- No man is an island, entire of itself; every man is a piece of the continent.
- I am a little pencil in the hand of a writing God who is sending a love letter to the world. —Paraphrased and attributed to Mother Teresa
- Thousands of candles can be lit from a single candle, yet the life of the candle will not be shortened. Happiness never decreases by being shared.
- Life is like riding a bike: To keep your balance you must keep moving.
- Once your heart's been broken, it grows back bigger.
- Worry is like a rocking chair: It keeps you busy, but gets you nowhere.
- The road to success is always under construction. —Arnold Palmer
- A successful man is one who can lay a firm foundation with bricks others have thrown at him.

- Yesterday is a cancelled check; today is cash on the line; tomorrow, a promissory note.
- Procrastination is the thief of time. — Edward Young
- Put your hand on a hot stove for a minute, and it seems like an hour. Sit with a pretty girl for an hour, and it seems like a minute. That's relativity. —Albert Einstein
- Don't let your victories get to your head, or your failures get to your heart.
- Here's one you can use anytime to state your case: "I'm on top of the world." When's the last time you told someone you were on top of the world? Picture yourself there for a moment right now. What are you doing? What brought you there? This is not a bad metaphor to use regularly. Why not get in the habit of telling people this? When people ask how we're doing, most of us respond with a nondescript "fine." This says nothing because it's what everybody says. **The next time someone asks you how you're doing, just tell them you're on top of the world. Maybe you are.** See what kind of reaction you get from them and from yourself.
- "I'm in the zone." In sports, the commentator often refers to a player in the zone as unconscious. Why? Because the player is "feeling it." He appears to be playing without thinking, as if he's just "channeling" energy and letting things happen, as if he's on autopilot. Peak performance comes when our inner critic goes silent and we're not giving and following directions in our head. We're just "being," being in the zone.
- Time is money. This statement infers a value of our time and the way we "spend" it. One of our greatest challenges is our management of our time. The number of distractions competing for our time is expanding at a record pace. Time management books and programs offer strategies to help us get things done with the time we have, and no doubt this is important, but there's also the question of living. If we're always "getting things done," but we aren't enjoying ourselves, we need to rethink what's happening with our lives.

We are not here to simply work through "to do" lists day after day. We need to ensure we are connecting the things on our list to the way we define ourselves. If everything we do on a daily basis is unrelated to how we define ourselves, as we discussed earlier, then we are spending too much time on things that don't really matter. This lack of focus will leave us unsatisfied and unfulfilled. **Time is more than money, and we have a limited amount of it, yet we carry on as if we have it in endless supply.** Time is life. It measures the passage of our lives. Can we remember to give time the reverence it deserves?

Let's look at some additional metaphors.

- I'm in a fog.
- I'm between a rock and a hard place.
- Cool as a cucumber
- The room is a disaster area.
- The fruit of knowledge
- She cut me down.
- Our eyes were glued to the scene.
- A heart of stone
- The heart of a lion
- Frozen with fear
- A shady character
- As sharp as a razor
- The light of my life
- The relationship turned sour.
- He's a dinosaur.

Think of an empowering metaphor for who you are. Here are a range of metaphors you can consider:

- A bullet train
- A light
- A waterfall
- A skyscraper
- A diamond
- A rocket ship
- A fire
- A satellite
- A whip
- A tiger
- An eagle
- A generator
- A beacon
- An explorer
- A laser
- A wheel

- A star
- A filter
- A bridge
- A river
- A fuse
- A piston
- A soldier

- A commander
- An interpreter
- A chameleon
- A furnace
- A rainstorm
- A symphony

Look at the list provided and feel free to make up your own list or add to this one. Now think of some of the challenges you face, and consider how you might approach a challenge if you thought of yourself as a generator, or a light, or a wheel, or any other metaphor. The idea is to prod yourself into considering new approaches to what may be constant challenges you face, such as maintaining your weight, staying focused on a project, or maintaining a positive relationship with someone. How could this concept be applied?

Let's take the challenge of maintaining a healthy weight. If I thought of myself as a filter, I might focus on my need to eat healthy food so I don't clog my filter. Natural foods digest easily while unnatural or processed foods take more work to digest, so they would tax my filter. Keeping this in mind might serve to keep me focused on the need to eat natural foods and avoid processed foods. If I thought of myself as a tiger, I could think about how essential it is to maintain myself so I could hunt effectively and be an efficient predator. While we don't actually hunt for our food these days, in one sense, it is necessary for us to maintain ourselves so that we can "hunt" effectively in the marketplace for the things we want. If I were a fire and I wanted to burn brightly, again I would think of how necessary it is to feed the fire good wood—good fuel—which would allow me to burn effectively.

These are three metaphors that give us different concepts, different visuals, for dealing with the same challenge. The possibilities here are endless. As you can see, every different model or metaphor you employ gives you a new approach. The more approaches you have to any given problem, the more likely you'll be successful. This reminds us again of the definition of insanity: doing the same thing over and over again and expecting a different result. This technique is geared to spur creativity, and this creates new neural pathways in the brain. And this allows us to be more effective, not only in facing a single challenge, but in everything.

Select two of your current challenges and apply three metaphors to each to spur your insight into facing these challenges. Write out your thoughts for each metaphor as applied to each challenge similar to the discussion above. DO THIS NOW.

Welcome back. You now have another technique that you can use to address any challenge, new or old, which you face. This technique has the added advantage of stretching your brain while you respond to your challenges. So, keep thinking and keep stretching.

Design Speed and Priority Mode

To effectively adopt the challenge identity, we must manage our time and our ability to generate and maintain momentum in reaching our objectives. I don't mean to alarm you . . . well, actually I do. We don't have forever. If yesterday's gone and tomorrow is promised to no one, then we really only have the present. This is not to say there's no value in planning for the future or learning from the past. Of course there is, but worrying about it gets you nothing but stress and the symptoms that come with it. There's no value in that. Nike has spent millions building an association with the phrase "Just do it." We can adopt "Do it now."

There is a do-it-now muscle in the brain located adjacent to the medulla oblongata, and like any other muscle in your body, it will atrophy and become powerless through lack of use. And like any other muscle, it can be built up in the same way we can develop biceps and triceps and core muscles. In our body, we have slow-twitch or slow-oxidative fiber muscles, such as postural muscles, and we have fast-twitch muscles, which are found in large numbers in the arms. The do-it-now muscle is very fast twitch and responds to training as well as any muscle in your body. In fact, once you start developing this muscle to full capacity, you'll find things getting done before you realize it. It starts taking on a life of its own. This is extremely productive.

Developing your do-it-now muscle doesn't necessarily mean you will be working harder. It does mean you'll be working smarter. I am sure you know of someone (yourself, myself) who has taken on projects and worked hard at them and yet the project languishes without completion. If you want to get something done, you need to make it a priority. Prioritizing is one of the most underappreciated skills there is. When you think of what you need to do on a given day, if you think of what it is most important to do and do that first, then you are not only developing your do-it-now muscle, you are maximizing its benefits and getting things done.

Prioritizing pushes the unimportant stuff out of the way by putting "first things first." Those unimportant things that previously prevented you from doing what you need to do may still be there, and you can still do them when there's time, you just can't do them now. Putting things off that you would rather do now is known as delayed gratification. The discipline to be able to delay gratification is an extremely valuable skill. **The greatest indicator of success is not talent. It's self-discipline.** Discipline is something everybody can develop. There are many talented people who never realize the benefits of their talents. I'm sure you can think of someone you know, or know of, who is an example of this. They just don't have the discipline to take advantage of their talents, to apply themselves, and to stay on task.

To develop your do-it-now muscle, we can start the way a weightlifter would train any muscle: light weights and multiple repetitions, light weights and multiple repetitions, light weights . . . you get the idea. Think of some simple task that you need to do on a regular basis but that you normally tend to put off. Resolve that you are going to use this task as your light weight to train on. Let's say you have a weekly task such as taking out the garbage on Monday night. (Any resemblance to the real world here is strictly coincidental.) You might have a habit of putting this off and occasionally forgetting to do it altogether. From now on, you're going to do it the first opportunity you have. And each time you do it, you're going to acknowledge that you're "working out," so to speak. Decide on your "task" and write down your commitment to do it at your first opportunity, whether it is a daily or weekly task. DO THIS NOW.

Where else can you apply this? Well, just about anywhere really, but remember we are starting with light weights and multiple repetitions, so pick more simple tasks to start with. The dishes, what about washing them first chance, as soon as you finish eating? Again, simple but reinforcing. Again, acknowledge this as part of your workout. Once you've begun to build some muscle tone, you can graduate to more involved tasks. If you're a student or you have work to bring home from your job, do it as soon as possible, or alternatively, set a specific time to do it. Say that the time is seven pm, get in the habit of starting a few minutes before your start time. Here again, instead of waiting the last few minutes until exactly seven, you're "jumping on it" and establishing your do-it-now identity.

The word "now" is an essential wheel for the successful identity. We not only want to get used to "do-it-now," we also want to be "in-the-now." For many of us, the problem is that so much of our self-talk doesn't have anything to do with what we're doing at a given moment. During our workday or our school day, we find ourselves thinking about what we didn't like about last weekend, or what we won't like about the coming weekend. The simple fact is that if we release these thoughts and focus on what we have to do at work or at school, we'll set ourselves up for a better weekend to come without even knowing it.

Now we can develop our prioritizing skills by starting each day with a list of the two most important things we want to accomplish that day. Write them down first thing in the morning, or even better, the night before, and then make sure you get to those tasks as soon as possible and check them off. Boom. Boom. Then, move on.

We also need to recognize the value of speed in tasking. I'm not suggesting we rush through things in a haphazard way, but we do need to think in terms of task movement and task completion. When something is done, let it be done. It's not necessary to agonize over every detail, playing out every possible option. Again, we don't have forever, so unless you want to spend the rest of your life working on whatever you are working on now, don't act like you have forever.

There's no better way to improve our lives than to get in the trenches and be in the moment. The moment. The moment. When you think about it, our lives are not made up of days or weeks or years. They are made up of moments. **We don't live a day at a time; we live a moment at a time.** When we break life down this way, everything becomes more manageable because you don't need to manage a day at a time, only a moment. When you conquer a moment, you set yourself up to conquer the next moment. One conquest leads to another. Too many times we might say to ourselves, "How am I going to get through today?" First of all, that's not an empowering question to ask. Secondly, you don't have to worry about getting through today. Just live this moment, and when this moment is over, go on to the next one. Simple enough, right? Right.

Here's an activity to build our in-the-moment synapses. Set your watch or phone alarm to go off every half-hour for as long as you can manage on a given day.

Go for at least three hours. Keep a notepad handy. Each time the alarm sounds, note your mood and rate yourself on a one-to-five-star scale as to how deeply you are in the moment, actually fully connected to what you're doing or what you're working on. The connection doesn't have to be limited to what you are doing physically.

For example, you could be mowing the lawn and you could be enjoying the physical activity and the weather, or you could be focused on working something through in your head such as writing a song. Either way, you could rate it as a five for being in the moment. But if you are worrying about how you're going to finish what you're doing and get to the bank before it closes or whatever else you still need to do, give yourself a one. This activity is about appreciating where you're at in a given moment. After all, at that moment, you're not anywhere else, so why not enjoy where you are. See if you can start piling up five-star moments. You're on the way to a five-star life.

Building on the knowledge that we don't have forever and we really are only guaranteed the present, we can work on our present awareness. This rating activity is a good start. Even better, work to have at least one moment of total release a day. Find one time each day where you can totally let go of your concerns, worries, faults, and fears, and just "be." Surely you're entitled to one moment a day. It can be in the middle of the most mundane task, or in a great conversation with a good friend. It is a moment of a realization that you're quite fine for the moment with where you are, where you "be." If you can find such a moment on a daily basis, the benefit of experiencing this feeling will resonate with you throughout the rest of your day. Just giving yourself this moment daily will be a gift, a gift that you give to yourself.

This is a moment of freedom and control at the same time. Freedom from your normal worries and mental chatter, and control in the sense that this is a moment you license to yourself to exercise full control in focusing and being in the present. There is a tremendous empowerment in this. In fact, if you can accomplish this, you can really accomplish anything because as you control your mind, you control your life, and what more could you ask for?

Each time you affirm and reinforce your ability to control your mind, you lay another brick in the foundational wall of your identity. And the pilot flying your ship is less troubled by shifts in the wind and the storms that will come.

Another condensed priority activity is to take an hour of your day at work and do a sixty-second prioritization. What one or two things do you really need to get done in the next sixty minutes? What would make this next hour successful? Write it . . . jot it down, and jump on it. When you set a priority and you have it in mind, it serves to filter the interruptions and the stopgap distractions that masquerade as urgent intrusions on your ability to do what you say you will do. You have an agenda. A man with focus and an agenda to attend to will get more done than a ship full of passengers. What do you need to do in the next sixty minutes? Write this down, and DO IT NOW.

So, challenges, obstacles, curves we face, all have to become our oxygen tanks, our rocket fuel, our growth pills. A day in which you're not challenged is a day you're not living. The challenge is to live well, to live well daily. When you adopt this approach, you begin to shoulder every burden with a positive first step. Without this approach, the first step is generally the hardest. Think of the quote above that points out that problems are like hills that appear steep from a distance but flatten out as we approach them.

Look at your current challenges. Here is an activity to gain perspective: Look at whatever challenge you consider to be your greatest obstacle at this moment. Now, think of some of the other great challenges you've dealt with in your lifetime. Perhaps they didn't turn out exactly as you wanted, but they didn't kill you either. I'm willing to bet you can find something equally or more challenging in your past that you survived. As you think of this past challenge, use this memory to remind yourself of your ability to survive whatever it is that you are facing now. Put these challenges side by side, and you're likely to find that anything you're dealing with now is not as difficult as something you've already faced. That gives you a good perspective to work with, to remind yourself that you can deal with whatever challenge you have now.

An ongoing challenge we need to embrace is the challenge of ongoing improvement. The question is what are we doing to make to make sure we're more today than we were yesterday. What are we doing to fuel our growth, our development?

While we're talking about improvement here, the drive for improvement needs to be built on the foundation of self-acceptance. If we fail to accept who we are then we have no meaningful foundation to build on. As we have emphasized earlier, we cannot afford to turn our lives into a chase to reach "someday" when we have everything we want because someday is a moving target. **Better to "be" the target than to chase it.** Better to recognize that we are just where we need to be, and step up from there, than to tell ourselves we'll begin to feel satisfied when we reach some point on the distant horizon.

That being said, let's continue our discussion of improvement. One place to start is any of our activities that are natural growth engines in the sense that they inherently involve challenge through ongoing participation, such as a sport, music, or art. I look at these as activities that naturally ask something more of us as we take them on. No matter what level we're at, we can always take things up a notch, to improve in some way when we engage in these activities. Let's say you play basketball. The next time that you play, ask yourself what part of your game you are going to improve. It could be your passing, or the follow-through on your jump shot, or your positioning for rebounding. You could select one aspect of your game for offense and one aspect for defense.

As we improve in any aspect of our life, we can build our confidence to improve every other aspect of our lives. We develop our ability to develop. You can choose your own acronym for this, such as your ability to BE (your Brilliant Evolution). Or for those of you who are music fans, it's your Brilliant Ongoing Wonderful and Intentional Evolution, your BOWIE. So, think of some thing or things that you can focus on improving, and build your awareness of these things.

As an example, I have recently come to realize that I have had a tendency to withhold praise in certain circumstances. Yet, in this book, I've made the point that making others feel good is a great thing to do, for yourself as well as others. Now, as I've focused on this, I find myself always looking to add something to a conversation that includes a compliment or praise of some sort. Often I look for an opportunity to acknowledge what someone has done for someone else. The beauty here is that this not only acknowledges someone so they can feel good, but it also reinforces their behavior of helping others. It's a way of paying it forward double time. Another example of win-win.

So, for the next week, look for at least two opportunities a day to praise someone for doing something for someone else. It can be as simple as saying, "It was great that you took the time to help your friend move her furniture." In one week, twice a day, this will give you fourteen chances to acknowledge someone. By the end of the week you'll start doing this without even thinking about it.

Now that we can see how healthy it is to have solid challenges in our lives, it's not a stretch to say we simply can't live without them. We can't grow without them. In fact, if our challenges are the only things we have to worry about, and we adopt the attitude that worry and dread are the opposite reaction to what we should have from a challenge, then it follows that we should be welcoming when they arise. We should be able to say, "Thank God, this is not what I would have originally wished for, but this will be good for me."

When you think about it, anything that could unsettle you or make you unhappy is a challenge, just by virtue of the fact that it makes you unhappy. So, if you now see the good to come from these challenges and can begin to truly welcome them, then you revolutionize your life. You kill worry by becoming welcoming.

Let's say you break your arm. You will now have to learn to function for a few months without using it as you normally would. This means you'll be forced out of your comfort zone and required to do things in ways that you haven't before. You also will not be able to do some things that you normally like to do for some period of time. Fine, that will push you to adapt and take up other activities to substitute for something you would regularly be doing.

I recently developed a case of tennis elbow. What to do? I started teaching myself to play left handed. Awkward at first, no doubt, but after repeated practice with hitting a foam ball against a wall, my strokes became more and more natural. I could feel the groove and the power of my strokes increase as I continued to practice. Every time we are pulled out of our comfort zone, we are pulled into a new way of being.

We may still, at times, come across a challenge we wish we didn't have. But wishing we had been able to sidestep a challenge doesn't get us anywhere. It's wishful thinking with no payoff. The principle of identity design is that we always design for power. **There is no power to be generated from wishing we didn't have a problem that we're facing.** As we now know, challenges are the treasure wrapped in silver-lined clouds. We need to keep flying through them. Enjoy the flight.

○━━ POINTS TO REMEMBER: ━━○

- Didn't the universe challenge you so you could grow stronger?
- We construct our reality as we perceive it.

- $\dfrac{\text{Event}}{\text{Perception}} = \text{Input} + \text{Identity} = \text{Response}$

- Thinking that the world is designed for our benefit is a powerful way to be.
- Praising intelligence praises what is, while praising effort praises the process of what one is becoming. We need a growth mindset.
- You want more power? Start looking for more challenges.
- Metaphors are powerful indicators of our attitudes. They pack a major punch in the world of self-talk.
- The next time someone asks you how you're doing, just tell them you're on top of the world. Maybe you are.
- Time is more than money, and we have a limited amount of it, yet we carry on as if we have it in endless supply.
- The greatest indicator of success is not talent. It's self-discipline.
- We don't live a day at a time, we live a moment at a time.
- Better to "be" the target than to chase it.
- There is no power to be generated from wishing we didn't have a problem that we're facing.

REJECTION AND FAILURE (THE SUCCESS TWINS)

Success consists of going from failure to failure with no loss of enthusiasm.
—Winston Churchill

Ever tried. Ever failed. No matter. Try Again. Fail again. Fail better.
—Samuel Beckett

*Most of my advances were by mistake. You uncover
what is when you get rid of what isn't.*
—R. Buckminster Fuller

Our greatest glory is not in never falling, but in rising every time we fall.
— Paraphrased and attributed to **Confucius**, among others

If we learn from our mistakes, why are we always so afraid to make a mistake?
—Anonymous

Failure is not an option. It's obligatory.
—**Judge Frank**

Rejection is a challenge.
—**Veronica Purcell**

The fact is if we want the life of our dreams, we need to develop a healthy relationship with rejection and failure. The word failure gets bandied about like the ultimate badge of shame. We hear people say things like "I don't want to be called a failure" and "Failure is not an option." But in reality, anybody who ever accomplishes anything, even the greatest of champions, fails along the way. So, warm up to failure because if you want to accomplish big things, then you're going to need to accept failures along the way.

In the history of sports and in our "winning is everything" culture, I'm not aware of anyone who ever won every game, or every event, or every championship they competed for. Roger Federer, the great tennis player who some call the greatest of all time, has won a record seventeen Grand Slam titles. Yet, he has competed in more than sixty Grand Slam events. Thus, perhaps the greatest tennis player ever failed more than two-thirds of the time. While we don't think of him as a failure, but rather as a champion, the plain fact is, he failed much more than he succeeded on this measure, and that's generally the way things are for anyone. **Failure precedes success.** Some people say you never really fail until you give up, and while there is some truth to that, I believe the healthiest approach is to simply accept that failure is part of the process and get on with it. In fact, we can say failure *is* the process. Trial and error.

In the history of the world, billions of people have learned to walk. No one, let me repeat, no one to my knowledge, ever learned how to walk without falling down. That's how we learn. We fall, we fail, we get up, we try again, and again, and again. You get the idea. How many times did you fall down learning to walk? When you learned to walk as a child, you saw people walking every day and you kept trying to "model" or "copy" them. You didn't care how many times you fell; you were focused on learning to walk.

What would your life have been like if you had reached, say fourteen months of age, and not yet learned to walk, and your parents had simply said, "Little Tommy has had enough failures, so we'll get him a wheelchair so he won't have the heartache of continuing to fail because he's had enough"? Hard to imagine. As a child, you did what you had to do to learn, and you didn't keep a scorecard or beat yourself up when you fell down. Can you say the same for yourself now?

What about learning to ice skate, or ski, or skateboard, or surf? Falling down is an important part of learning to do any of these things. Actually, the more comfortable you are with falling down, the quicker you learn. Why is that? For one thing, fear makes any task more difficult because it inhibits our ability to learn freely. Fear makes us tense, and when we are tense, we lose a measure of our dexterity and our ability to perform. Our basic coordination is impaired. Secondly, these are all tasks that are built on the skill of balance. To learn, you have to push yourself past the level of skill that you have, and the only sure way to do that is to push yourself to the point where you fall, the point where you fail. Just as we are designed to learn, we are designed to fail as we learn, and there's no shame in that, unless you choose to say there is. (Why do I keep referencing choices and mentioning the "choose" word? Because that's where the action is. **Making choices is our design factory.**) Our identity needs to welcome failure just as we need to welcome learning. It's all a natural part of the process of growth. Any life worth living is going to be a life full of growth.

Thomas Edison, the great inventor, is said to have tried 10,000 times in various experiments to perfect the electric light. When he was asked, "How did it feel to fail 10,000 times?" he replied, "I don't feel like I failed 10,000 times. I just found 10,000 ways that didn't work." Clearly, he had a plan to invent the electric light, and he believed he could do it. He was willing to give as much time and effort as it would take. He didn't see his misses as failures, only as steps to success. Successful people don't necessarily think of their efforts as "failures," they think of "outcomes." Edison's 10,000 outcomes weren't the ones that he wanted so he kept going until he got the outcome he was after.

Columbus sailed off to find a new route to the Indies. As he sailed west each day and saw nothing but water ahead of him, he could have accepted that he had failed and turned back. But each day of "failure" was a day that brought him closer to where he was going. His motto may have been "I have to sail to fail . . . to succeed." He was apparently comfortable enough with the thought that he wasn't there yet, but he was on his way. That concept can serve as a lesson for all of us.

Let's take a look at some key points from someone's life history as stated by author Anthony Robbins. See if you can guess who this is.

This individual:

- Failed in business at age thirty-one.
- Lost a state legislature race at age thirty-two.
- Failed again in business at thirty-four.
- Had a nervous breakdown at age thirty-six.
- Lost an election at age thirty-eight.
- Lost a congressional election at age forty-three.
- Lost a congressional election at age forty-six.
- Lost a congressional election at age forty-eight.
- Lost a senatorial election at age fifty-five.
- Failed in an effort to become vice president at age fifty-six.
- Lost a senatorial race at age fifty-eight.
- Was elected president of the United States of America at age sixty.

The man's name?

It was Abraham Lincoln. How do you think he looked at his losses? He is now remembered as one of the greatest presidents of all time. How different would our history be if he had simply said, "I've had enough of failures," and given up on politics instead of running for president.

Then there's Michael Jordan, the basketball player. Arguably the greatest basketball player ever, Jordan was once cut from his high school team. He remembers his share of failures. "I have missed more than 9,000 shots in my career. I have lost almost 300 games. On 26 occasions, I have been entrusted to take the game-winning shot, and I missed. **I have failed over and over and over again in my life. And that is why I succeed.**"

Many of the most successful entrepreneurs in the world started out as repeat failures. Henry Ford, the fabulously successful founder of Ford Motor Company, revolutionized manufacturing with his innovative assembly line. He is also recognized for paying high wages to his employees so they could afford the cars they were producing. But his early businesses failed, and he went broke five times before he broke through, creating one of the most iconic brands in the world today.

R.H. Macy, the founder of the Macy's department store chain, started seven businesses that failed before he founded the successful retail giant. Stephen King's first book, *Carrie*, was rejected thirty times until he actually threw the manuscript in the trash. His wife fished it out and convinced him to resubmit it. King is now one of the bestselling authors of all time. Vincent van Gogh sold only one painting during his lifetime, and it was to a friend. Now his paintings are among the most well-known and most valuable in the world.

Think of your fears. Surely you have fears that involve a fear of failure of one sort or another. **Allowing fear of failure to hold us back is a luxury we simply cannot afford if we intend to claim the life of our dreams.** Just as we discussed fear and how it impacts our ability to learn to balance for balance sports such as skating, the tension of fear inhibits our ability to do anything to the best of our abilities because it saps our focus. Anything that detracts from our focus is going to impact our ability to learn and to perform.

Another factor in this chapter is a phenomenon called "risk aversion," which refers to the tendency of people to strongly prefer to avoid suffering a loss rather than acquiring a gain. This results in risk aversion because any risk naturally involves some potential loss even if it is only a loss of time or effort. So if we plan to be bold, we need to recognize that loss and risk aversion may push us to "stay put."

This principle of risk or loss aversion has been employed as a motivator in a program in the Chicago Heights Public Schools. Some teachers were given a bonus at the beginning of the year with the understanding that they would have to pay part of it back if student performance did not improve. Others were told they would earn a bonus to be paid at the end of the year. The teachers who were given the prepaid bonus outperformed their colleagues who were given the traditional bonus, with gains that were two to three times higher in student performance. It was interesting to see that merely restructuring that format of the bonus, without actually changing the amount at stake, made such a significant difference. If this "loss aversion in reverse" can make ordinary teachers into superteachers, we need to know the power that loss aversion can have in keeping us from pursuing our dreams.

The "framing effect" is another example of loss aversion at work. People respond differently when a question is framed in a negative versus a positive approach. For example, Amos Tversky and Daniel Kahneman looked at how different phrasing affected responses to a hypothetical life or death situation. Participants were asked to consider two different treatments for individuals suffering from a deadly disease. First, treatment A was presented from a negative standpoint. Of 600 people affected by the disease, treatment A would result in 400 deaths. Treatment B had a 33 percent chance that no one would die and a 66 percent chance that everyone would die. Then, the choice was framed from a positive standpoint. Treatment A would "save" 200 lives and treatment B had a 33 percent chance of saving everyone and a 66 percent chance of saving no one. They found that 72 percent of participants chose treatment A when it was presented with positive framing (200 lives would be saved). Only 22 percent chose treatment A when it was presented with negative framing (400 people would die).

In another example, 93 percent of PhD students registered early when faced with a penalty fee for late registration while only 67 percent did so when this was identified as a discount for early registration. This should settle any remaining doubts you might have that word choice matters.

When we do fail at something, the key to being productive is to make sure that we get something out of it.

Let's look at some possible responses to failure:

1. You can curse your fate. "I failed, this is bad news, it's terrible, and this sucks."
2. You can curse your fate and question your ability and your self-image. "I failed. This is bad. Can't I ever do anything right?"
3. You can give up. "I failed. I'm never going to try something like this again."
4. You can look for the lesson you've earned. "I failed. This didn't turn out the way I wanted it to. What can I learn from this? What can I do differently the next time?"

When we break it down this way, it's fairly obvious what the best approach is. Let's see if you can identify some failures you've experienced and some lessons you've learned. Can you identify three "failures"? State the failure and what you have learned from it. State how you felt about it when it occurred and how you feel about this now. Write this out. DO THIS NOW.

In fact, writing about any traumatic event, whether it relates to some failure on your part or some trauma or loss you've suffered, has been shown to boost mental and physical well-being, self-esteem, and happiness. Writing has been deemed more effective than simply talking about a traumatic event. Writing can call forth a sense of focus not always present when someone simply talks about an experience. Many of our treatment programs for young people at court include writing activities for just this reason. Benefits have been seen even when writing as little as a few minutes a day. This phenomena and related research is discussed by Richard Wiseman in *59 Seconds*. Now, look back at what you've written. Can you see the benefit you've received, the development to your character that has come from these experiences?

This activity should get you to feel more comfortable with failure, and to recognize that it's a step toward success. It should help you recognize that failure is part of your journey. It should help you to start looking at failure the way Thomas Edison and Abraham Lincoln did. We don't aim to fail. We aim to move on, and failure is part of what happens along the way. If we don't ever fail at anything, we're just not pushing ourselves. We're likely doing the same things over and over again.

The fact is the more risks we take, the better we get at taking risks. Accepting risk is a power move that creates possibilities. While it's true that one of those possibilities is failure, this comes with the territory and is part of the process. In the eyes of someone like Thomas Edison, it's really not failure at all, it's an outcome. Now, let's look at another aspect of this failure phenomenon. Think of something that you failed at initially, and then persevered and eventually achieved. This could be something in school, or sports, or work, or any field of your life. DO THIS NOW.

We can break this down further. Think about what your thoughts were at the time of your initial failure, and what you did to persevere to eventually accomplish what you were working to achieve. Write this out. DO THIS NOW.

This is a great activity for designing your identity because it acknowledges you as someone with a growth mindset rather than a talent mindset, as we discussed above. A growth mindset puts you in position to learn and adapt to improve your outcomes and your life. It acknowledges you as a "can do" person.

The twin sister of failure is rejection. Reject means to refuse to accept, and rejection is the action or state of being rejected. Haven't we all been rejected in different ways over the years? Let's take a closer look at this notion of rejection. Jack Canfield, the cocreator of the *Chicken Soup for the Soul* book series, has written a brilliant book called *The Success Principles* that includes a wonderful discussion of rejection. (Is that an oxymoron, a "wonderful discussion of rejection"?) He can certainly speak from experience. He and his partner, Mark Victor Hansen, decided they wanted to publish a book that simply told great stories with a positive theme. They approached over one hundred publishers before they found someone to publish the first book.

All of the publishers who turned them down didn't think this book would sell, but Jack and Mark disagreed and they didn't give up. (This was back in the not-too distant past, when you actually needed a publisher to sell a book. Now, you just need an Internet connection.) They found a publisher and now have sold over one hundred million copies of the series. They applied the same effort to marketing their books as they did to finding a publisher and now, one hundred million copies later, life is pretty good for Jack Canfield and Mark Victor Hansen and for millions of people who have enjoyed the inspirational stories in these books. So, the next time you do something and it doesn't come out the way you wanted, just recognize that you created an outcome, and if it wasn't the outcome you intended, then accept the lesson the Lord intended you to learn from the experience and keep going.

As for rejection, as Jack Canfield points out, rejection itself is just a myth. It's just something we make up in our mind. Think about it. If you apply for a job and you don't get it, nothing really happened to change your circumstances. You didn't have the job before you applied, and you don't have it after you applied. If you ask someone for a date and they say no, you weren't going on a date with them before you asked them and you're not going on one after you asked. Nothing really changed. But if you never ask, you never give yourself a chance. So when you want something, don't be afraid to ask for it. You really have nothing to lose. And what people consider to be rejection, like failure, is just part of the process.

Consider SWSWSWSW which, as stated by Mr. Canfield, stands for "Some will, some won't, so what, someone's waiting." In other words, if you want something, let's say a date for a concert, or a partner for a project, recognize that you might have to ask more than one person. In fact, you might have to ask a lot of people and hear the word "no" multiple times. Many times life is a numbers game, and you have to get through a lot of "nos" before you get the yes that you want. So, how many "nos" can you take?

How many times have you failed to ask for something you wanted just because you didn't want to hear that little word no? It's actually one of the smallest words in the English language, two letters and one syllable. The word itself has no power other than that which you choose to give it. As Anthony Robbins says, "Success is buried on the other side of rejection," and "There are no real successes without rejection." The more rejection you get, the better you are, the more you've learned, and the closer you are to what you want. The next time you hear the word no, you can simply say thank you.

We're building an identity to get the life we want. That doesn't mean we're never going to hear the word no. It means when we hear it, we realize **the word no is simply part of the symphony of life.** We adopt our own translation; no can simply mean not yet, not at this time.

The key issue most of us have with experiencing failure or rejection is our concern with what other people think. What will people say if I fail? Won't I look like a fool? Why should I subject myself to that? You might think these are natural concerns that everyone has. But what about the child learning to walk? Have you ever seen a one-year-old learning to walk stop and fall down out of fear of what everyone will say? No. That tells us that this "fear" is a learned fear that we adopt as we grow older. What sense does it make to live your life according to what other people think? None. Even if they were to think you did make a fool of yourself, will they even remember whatever you did a week from now, or even a day from now? You might say, "But it's embarrassing." But is it? Why? Because you choose to be embarrassed?

Dr. Albert Ellis, recognized as one of the most influential psychologists of the twentieth century, developed an approach with Dr. Aaron Beck, which came to be known as cognitive-behavioral therapy. Rather than working to help his clients *talk* through their problems, he trained them to *work* through them. Daniel Coyle, in his book *The Talent Code*, discussed Dr. Ellis's philosophy: "The trouble with most therapy is that it helps you feel better. But you don't get better. You have to back it up with action, action, action." In his shyness clinics, he had clients start out with simple conversational exercises and work up to tasks that involved situations of planned embarrassment, such as dropping a watermelon on the floor in the middle of a crowded supermarket. This watermelon butterfingers exercise is designed to expose individuals to embarrassing circumstances so they can overcome them. If you have a fear of embarrassment that's holding you back, you might want to try fumbling a few watermelons yourself to thicken your skin so you can eliminate this as a concern.

Other people live other lives. No one spends twenty-four hours a day in your head, in your skin, like you do. No one was born with the unique set of talents and drives that you have. No one sees the world exactly the way you do, so why bother to worry about what they think? Look, you're not going to reach any real level of satisfaction on your deathbed, with your final breaths, being able to say, "Well, at least I made it through life, and no one never thought I made a fool of myself." At what cost? Your dreams? No, that's as ridiculous as it sounds.

Accepting failure as part of the symphony or process of life can free us from the mountains of worry and stress that fear of failure generates. If we recognize that we could fail, and that it won't be the end of the world, and that we don't have to beat ourselves up over it, we find that we've eliminated a major source of stress. And less stress means more success. All of us who have played sports or games in our lifetime have lost or failed at one time or another. In the bigger picture of things, what difference did it make? Life is the game as we see it.

Anytime we hold ourselves back because of this fear, it's like a player refusing to take the field in a game. You can't win if you're not on the field. The risk of failure and what people might say is no reason to live your life on the sideline. It didn't stop Thomas Edison. It didn't stop Abraham Lincoln. It didn't stop Jack Canfield. There are literally millions of other successful people who put themselves on the field, took their lumps, and kept on going, recognizing that they couldn't win unless they were open to the fact that they could lose, that they could fail. And when they did, they could dust themselves off and have another go at it. The process says we will fail, and we will fall, as we make our way in this world. And each time we do, we have one more reminder that we are pushing ourselves into new territory. We are closing in on the life of our dreams.

○⊂⊃ **POINTS TO REMEMBER:** ⊂⊃○

- Failure precedes success. It's part of the process.
- Making choices is our design factory.
- *I have failed over and over and over again in my life. And that is why I succeed.* — Michael Jordan
- Allowing fear of failure to hold us back is a luxury we simply cannot afford if we intend to claim the life of our dreams.
- The word no is simply part of the symphony of life.
- Accepting failure as part of the symphony or process of life can free us from the mountains of worry and stress that fear of failure generates.

IDENTITY STATE
(WHAT A STATE YOU'RE IN)

All human behavior is a result of the state we're in.
—Anthony Robbins

The quality of your life is the quality of your movement.
—Moshe Feldenkrais (paraphrased)

Your intellect may be confused, but your emotions will never lie to you.
—Roger Ebert

When I say manage your emotions, I only mean the really distressing, incapacitating emotions. Feeling emotions is what makes life rich. You need your passions.
—Daniel Goleman

I went through this realization that acting, at its heart, is the ability to manipulate your own emotions.
—Scarlett Johansson

When we direct our thoughts properly, we can control our emotions.
—W. Clement Stone

S tate is defined as a mode or condition of being. We have many. We have powerful states and powerless states. Pleasant and playful, productive and passive, peaceful and pugnacious, and on, and on. Our state is crucial to how we feel at any moment and how we react to what happens around us. If we want to maximize our power and effectiveness, we need to seize state control. We need to manage our emotions, master our moods, and develop our ability to shift from an undesirable state to a desirable one.

Do you think you can be more powerful, more effective, by managing your emotions and mastering your moods? Well, of course, why are we asking such an obvious question? First of all, because the question itself is empowering, and second, it points us toward our destination: state control. There is a key to the empowerment of this question. Look at it. More power and more effectiveness from what? From managing things that are yours. We are talking about your emotions and your moods. Not somebody else's. **The beauty is nobody can exercise more control over your emotions and your moods than you can. And the payoff is massive.** This discussion confirms your place at the center of your universe, reinforcing the power you have over yourself. Because when you seize state control, you place yourself precisely where you want to be.

The fact is if you don't take control of your state, as many people don't, you simply fall into the random pattern (is that an oxymoron?) of bouncing from state to state, reacting to what goes on around you, what you see on the news, what your friends say, what you read in the magazines, what you hear on the radio. Is that any way to live? The identity we're building here demands more power, thus control is necessary.

There are optimum states for various tasks. What is a great state for one task could be less valuable or even disabling for another. If you are working to learn to play a piece of music that you don't know, you would be better served by a more focused cerebral state than if you were performing a well-known piece of music for a live audience. In performance mode, you are better served to be more emotionally charged and less matter of fact. A live audience will feed off the energy of a performer; this energy is absent when someone is in learning mode. So, when we think about state, one of the first questions is what state are we looking for. For whatever you are doing, consider what the state is that will help you maximize your effort and enjoyment.

When we think about evolution, we might think that we would have naturally evolved in such a way that our minds are always in their optimum state. Why not? Isn't the maxim of evolution "survival of the fittest"? Unfortunately, it hasn't worked out that way. The mind is a wonderful thing, but the ability to feel depressed, frustrated, or just plain bored or bothered, seems to have outmuscled the ability to feel enchantment for many. Has this happened to you?

Think about your mindset as you go through the day. How much of your day do you spend upbeat as opposed to downbeat? Without any specific plan or design, our moods fluctuate with the infinite number of variables we face in daily life. The news, the weather, the traffic, a song, a memory, a friend's comment, all of these can shift us from one state to another before we know it. To get in touch with your state frequency—the general amount of time you spend in various states—you can journal for a day. Journal what you do and how you feel, or what state you're in as you do it.

Another way to develop your appreciation for the importance of state is to start analyzing the states of others as they deal with various challenges or tasks. For the next week, assess the state of some friend, family member, or colleague as you work or associate with them. Consider whether they are or are not in a resourceful state for whatever it is that they are doing. You can rate them in your mind on a scale of one to ten for how effective you believe their state is. Ask them outright how they feel about what they're doing, or how they would rate themselves. Maybe you can even suggest some adjustment that will help them be more effective. People are always interested in themselves, so when you talk to them about how they're doing, you'll be covering their favorite topic.

The field of sports psychology has exploded as athletes look for every edge to achieve the optimal mindset to perform their best. There are specialists brought in to work with athletes, not to teach technique, fitness or game strategy, but strictly to help individuals develop and apply the right mental skills to harness their best performance state. If you were to hire a "performance consultant," think of which of the following credentials or skills would be most helpful in deciding who would be best able to help you to do your best.

Someone who:

- Is highly invested in seeing you achieve your best results
- Knows your background better than anyone else
- Can tune in to you so well it's as though they can read your mind
- Knows exactly what fears you have and what motivates you
- Is willing to adapt and use different strategies when necessary
- Is experienced in assisting others in personal transformation

All of these factors in a personal coach would serve you well. Think about who you know who would best fit this description. Who would be your top candidate to fill this position?

The fact is no one can match this description. No one can serve this role better than you. The concept of identity design is that we need to develop to be the best personal coach we can be so that we can coach ourselves to be at our best. No one has more at stake here than we do. No one else has more to gain or more to lose. You may not feel you have a great deal of experience in helping others with their personal transformation, but maybe this would be a good time to start. Helping others transform and find the best in themselves will help you do the same.

The next time you want to adopt a particular state, let your memory go to work and take a moment to recall a prior occasion when you were in that state. Use this to lift you to where you want to be. You can also visualize, or imaginize, everything turning out exactly as you would like as you perform with complete confidence.

I'm sure you've heard people say things such as "I'm having a bad day," or "I'm having a bad week." **The fact is there's no such thing as a bad day. We don't live a week at a time, or even a day, or an hour, or a minute at a time. We live a moment at a time.** You can have a bad moment, but a moment is just that, and it's gone before you know it, and here you are as a new moment begins.

Your state can change from moment to moment. Think of the things that can change your state. You're driving home from work after a challenging day, and a favorite song that you haven't heard in ages comes on the radio and you pump up the volume and sing along. You experience an instant change of state.

Or a friend you haven't heard from in months calls you to catch up, and you start talking about that college canoe trip from years ago when you camped for four days, living on hot dogs and Fruit Loops. Neither of these things changes the condition of your life in any significant way, yet they dramatically change your state. Why?

State is an internal phenomenon. State is not dependent upon whether it's raining or snowing, or day or night, or hot or cold. Some people prefer rain, some snow. Take farmers and snowboarders, for example. We are unable to summon rain or snow at will, but we can discipline ourselves to summon moods, or modes, at will. This is what an actor does when they play a scene. If the scene is one in which an actor witnesses the death of a parent, they will think of when they suffered a great loss and create the appropriate "state" that the scene calls for. They could not effectively play the scene while thinking about their favorite comedy.

Our basic brain units are the neurons, and there are about one hundred billion of these in our brain. Neurons are cells that transmit information through electrical and chemical signals. A chemical signal travels via a synapse, a specialized connection with other cells. Each of these neurons has thousands of connections with other neurons, and as a result, there are trillions of neural connections in the brain. These are roads or pathways for our thoughts. Brain research has established the malleability of the brain. No matter what age we are, our brain has the ability to forge new connections and discard old ones. The more deeply ingrained a pattern is, the more it takes to undo it, but the liberating fact here is that we are only prisoners to our thoughts if we allow ourselves to be.

Stroke victims suffer disruptions to neural pathways that disable their ability to walk or talk. Rehabilitation therapy with these individuals builds new neural pathways, allowing them to relearn these basic functions. Since more than two-thirds of strokes afflict individuals sixty-five and over, it's easy to see that advanced age doesn't prevent this redevelopment. The ability of the brain to reinvent pathways is part of what is referred to as neuroplasticity. There's an empowering concept for us—our brains are plasticlike, hmmm.

Let's take a look at what happens when we choose to change a pattern of behavior. We have an established pattern of thought, a highway connection of neurons in our brain. This pattern leads us to eat ice cream as an evening snack between seven and eight pm. If we are home at this time, this is what we do and the pathway is well established. We've decided this would be a good habit to break, and we've thought about doing it, but we haven't yet acted to vary the pattern.

Taking what we know about neurons, we're going to hire some road builders. We want to build a new highway that leads to a more beneficial type of behavior than the cookies-and-cream freeway we've been frequenting. Our ice cream habit might be seen as a reward we indulge in for completing another day's work. We're looking to build a substitute road so we should look for a substitute reward. We could choose to take five or ten minutes to retreat to a place where we could listen to some favorite music, uninterrupted, with the design that we are going to so thoroughly enjoy ourselves that it will be better than eating a bowl full of double chocolate marshmallow fudge.

This might sound like a stretch, but the fact is stranger things than this have worked. And, of course, the first few days you're going to choose some of your absolute favorite music. The heavy lifting in establishing your new pathway is right off the bat because each time you succeed in reaching for the headphones instead of the spoon, that new pathway becomes stronger and deeper, and the old one begins to wither away. In a month, you'll have effectively rewired your brain.

Medical research has confirmed the mind/body connection, and it's important for us to realize this connection and its implications to our discussion of state. In 1975, Professor Robert Ader, who later literally wrote the book *Psychoneuroimmunology*, in this new field, made a discovery that many consider central to establishing the link between mind and body for the immune system. He was investigating conditioned response (the old Pavlov's dog, bell and saliva concept). He was testing to see how long a conditioned response could last in laboratory rats by using a combination of saccharine-laced water and the nausea-inducing drug Cytoxan. He trained the rats to associate the sweet solution with a bad bellyache, which was caused by the Cytoxan. After conditioning the rats, he gave them saccharine water without the Cytoxan and watched to see how long it would take for them to forget the connection between the two.

Unexpectedly, in the second month, the rats started to die off from disease. Puzzled by this development, Ader researched the properties of the nausea-inducing Cytoxan and learned that one of its side effects was an immune suppressant. The rats had been conditioned to associate the sweet water with not only nausea, but with a shutdown of their immune systems. The conclusion was clear: Their minds were controlling their immune systems. (Kathy Quinn Thomas. "The Mind-BODY Connection: Granny Was Right, After All." University of Rochester, *Rochester Review*, Spring-Summer 1995.)

You are surely aware of the fact that your emotions play a major role in driving your behavior. Our brains are wired to seek and respond to threats and rewards. When we detect one of these, the brain releases chemicals that travel through the body, resulting in the feelings we refer to as our emotions. Threats result in the release of the stress hormones, adrenaline or cortisol, which prepares us for fight or flight. Rewards, such as acknowledgment for an achievement or good behavior by a child, cause the release of dopamine, oxytocin, or serotonin, the "feel good" messengers. Sometimes our emotions are so deep and immediate that we lose the ability to think rationally in the moment. We are overcome by our feelings.

What to do? We can manage our emotions, our feeling brain, and its effects at the subconscious level by managing our conscious thoughts. Our conscious thoughts can be a two-edged sword. We can create stress and cause the release of the stressor hormones simply by thinking about a possible threat. We commonly refer to this as "worrying about what might happen." The problem with worrying about what might happen is that it focuses our expectations on negative circumstances and outcomes. Expectations lead to outcomes. You've heard the expression that you can be your own worst enemy. For my money, truer words were never spoken. And this is it. Stress is defined as mental tension or worry. Worry releases our stress hormones, and we start to spend so much time and attention worrying about what could happen that we practically will it into existence. And even if what we worry about doesn't happen, we've inflicted damage on ourselves just by worrying about what might happen.

Sustained release of cortisol, caused by stress, suppresses the immune system, increases blood pressure, and impairs learning and memory retrieval. Adrenaline also impairs immune function and increases heart rate. Health problems associated with ongoing activation of the stress response system and the release of these hormones include heart disease, sleep problems, digestive problems, depression, obesity, and various skin conditions. (For more information you can look at "Stress: Constant Stress Puts Your Health at Risk" by the Mayo Clinic Staff. MayoClinic. org.) Just look at this list of health problems associated with stress. This is nasty stuff. Inability to sleep, or eat, obesity. Stress is a killer. These are the symptoms that make it a killer.

Science has provided substantial data detailing how negative emotions harm the body. Sustained stress or fear creates wear and tear on the body's biological systems and leads to illnesses such as heart disease, stroke, and diabetes. Chronic anger and anxiety disrupt cardiac function through changes in the heart's electrical stability. Jack P. Shonkoff, professor of pediatrics at Harvard, reports on the damage of "toxic stress," the continued activation of the body's stress response system that results from early life experiences such as chronic neglect and exposure to violence. These experiences damage the brain and other organ systems in the body, and the effects include a hair-trigger response that can lead to a faster heart rate, higher blood pressure, and a spike in stress hormones. (See Sara Rimer, journalist, and Madeline Drexler, editor. "Happiness and Health." *HSPH News* Winter 2011. HSPH.Harvard.edu.)

Stress is a killer, a silent killer. All of this damage is being done internally. While it can be triggered by an event or an incident that happens to us, the ongoing damage is inflicted not by what is happening to us at any given moment, but by our memory of what happened to us in the past, and the effect of that memory on ourselves.

In our juvenile court, we hear victim impact statements from survivors of violent crime. I heard from a college student who was lured into the woods and robbed by individuals who threatened him and cut him with a knife, and then forced him to strip to his underwear—no doubt a terrifying experience. Months after the incident, he reported being unable to drive, keeping his blinds drawn at all times, and suffering ongoing anxiety. This is the kind of stress and the kind of damage that can result from a single violent incident. In other cases, we hear from individuals who no longer feel safe in their home of twenty years or more after suffering a break-in.

These are extreme, though unfortunately not isolated, incidents. We have communities riddled with crime, and some of the worst are zip codes that fall within the jurisdiction of our court. Whether it's an episode of violence, or a more generalized fear or worry about what might happen, the fact is when we look at our bodies' response to stress and all the nasty things that come with it, we need to contain it. We need to kill it before it kills us. In a sense, it's like smoking.

Nobody dies from smoking a single cigarette, or from a moment of stress, but as time marches on and smoking and stress continue, scars appear on the lungs of smokers, and those who suffer from toxic stress fall victim to stroke and heart disease and all of the other health risks listed above.

If stress and negative emotions can make us ill, this would suggest there could be health benefits to having a positive mental attitude and emotions. Laura Kubzansky, a Harvard associate professor of Society, Human Development, and Health, has been engaged in research tackling this very issue. "In a 2007 study that followed more than 6,000 people aged 25 to 74 for 20 years, she found that emotional vitality—a sense of enthusiasm, of hopefulness, of engagement in life, and the ability to face life's challenges with emotional balance—appears to reduce the risk of coronary heart disease. The protective effect was distinct and measurable." She has also documented "that children who are able to stay focused and on task and are optimistic at age seven report better overall health and fewer illnesses 30 years later. Her findings indicate that optimism cuts the risk of coronary heart disease by 50 percent." (See Sara Rimer, journalist, and Madeline Drexler, editor. "Happiness and Health." *HSPH News* Winter 2011. HSPH.Harvard.edu.)

Given what we've discussed above, this is exactly what we should expect to find. If the stress of negative thoughts makes us unhealthy, then it's natural to expect optimism to bring greater overall health. What this all points to is that if you want to be healthy, you need to be happy. Emotional health predicts physical health. This makes our quest to design a powerful and confident identity all the more urgent. Our health is at stake. **Emotional health and joy will not only bring us better days, they will bring us more of them.**

Changing state basically comes down to one of two things. You can change your thoughts or change your stance. We can go "inside out" or "outside in." Let's look at the inside out approach first. In thoughts, we can change what we are thinking about or how we are looking at something. If we've just lost a great friend, we can focus on the fact that we will never see them again, or if they were gravely ill, we can focus on the fact that they will no longer be suffering. Same subject, but a different focus. We could also change what we're thinking about altogether.

Our state relates to what we choose to use our willpower to focus on. We need to hold the belief that anything that can be done through willpower is 100 percent within our control. And why not? Anything less is a sellout. Anything less shortchanges our own ability to think. Why would you do that? Why would we want to accept that someone else can think a certain way and we can't? That would be accepting the fact that we are mentally crippled. We're talking about willpower (not intelligence), the simple intention of doing something or not doing something.

Winifred Gallagher discusses in her book *Rapt* that our life really comes down to one thing: Our life is what we pay attention to. We need to pay attention to how we are "spending" our most valuable resource, our attention. Every moment of every minute is a moment that we can choose what we are paying attention to. The sad fact is that in today's modern world, with more "devices" sending more messages of the mundane and the meaningless our way in a steady stream, we are surrendering our attention without a fight. What began with the television has exploded exponentially to the point that many of us seem willing to simply accept that our lives are always somewhat beyond our control because there's so much damn "stuff" to deal with. The fact is we don't have to accept this for a minute. **We just need to pay attention to what we pay attention to.**

Ms. Gallagher relates how her decision to write a book on the subject of what we pay attention to was triggered by her own monumental midlife crisis. Walking out of the hospital after receiving news of what she calls the "biopsy from hell" (a diagnosis of a severely aggressive cancer), she concluded that rather than let the disease monopolize her attention, she would focus on living her life instead.

What did she do with her months of chemo, surgery, more chemo, and daily radiation? She focused on the present and on the things that made her feel the best. She focused on her family and friends, her spiritual life and her work, as well as on smaller favors such as movies, walks, and martinis. She found that by focusing on whatever seemed meaningful, productive, or energizing, and avoiding negative and destructive thoughts, she was able to carry on and "pretty much" remain in good spirits. At first blush, this seems to be a remarkable reaction for someone living under the cloud of a near death sentence, but is it? While we have to admire Ms. Gallagher for forgoing the pity party, the fact is that her reaction is not unique. Many people we have come to admire are people who have responded to trouble with grace under pressure.

To manage our state, we can use an "inside out" approach or an "outside in" approach. Let's talk about how we're going to exercise control over our state with the inside out approach. We're going to experience a variety of states and we're going to need to be able to shift from negative to positive. We need a strategy to go from suffering or doubt, to peace or confidence, from boredom to enchantment, from anger to calm. How?

For those of you with children, you've probably used the distraction technique. Kids wear their emotions on their sleeve, so we can break down a change of state in a child, and apply the lesson of what we see externally with kids to the work we need to do internally with ourselves. Your son skins his knee and starts crying like he just broke a leg and lost four quarts of blood. If you tell him, "You're okay," and offer comfort, what happens? If your child is like mine, he keeps on crying. He's in a negative state, so his upset and tears are creating a vicious circle. Offering comfort can actually reinforce this state as you shower your son with love and affection in response to the trauma of his skinned knee and his current state. He senses your concern and offer of comfort as a confirmation that something has gone wrong. And if you're very concerned, he knows something has gone drastically wrong.

What to do? One option is to go for the distracting change of state. In a voice filled with astonishment, you say, "What's that . . . out the window . . . I can't believe it . . . is that a raccoon?" As soon as he looks up, he's forced to stop crying if he wants to see what you're talking about. Since there's actually nothing unusual out the window for him to see, you start chattering about the raccoon that just darted out of sight right out from under your noses, and how big and fast it was, and how you can't believe it and neither can he, and before he can realize what's happened as he tries to picture this oversized raccoon you're talking about, with the blinding speed and the titanic tail, guess what? You've broken his state, and there's no going back. He can't simply go back to crying like he was.

You've shifted his focus out of the pattern he was running. You torpedoed it. How did you do this? You changed what he was thinking about. You changed what he was focusing on. This doesn't only work with kids. A friend of mine has to deal with an aunt who loves to complain and rant and whine. Once she gets started in on something, she grinds away mercilessly. When this is a phone call, my friend will feign an interruption. It's like pulling a wheel off a well-oiled machine. Her aunt has to wait until she gets back on the phone or calls back, and the momentum of the destructive cycle is broken. Even if she still wants to complain, she can't manage the same intensity as she had before the interruption.

Can you distract yourself? Can you hang up on yourself? Sure. You just need the mental equivalent of a bucket of cold water. You just need to be able to wrench your mind from what's bothering you to something else. You need a change of focus. You could even literally say out loud, "I'm sick of thinking of this. I'm hanging up on myself. I'm going to start thinking about _____."

Here's an activity you can do to facilitate state change and develop your ability to understand and execute it. Set out two lists of memories, one positive and one negative. Concentrate first on a negative memory. Think about it . . . let the burden of it infuse you . . . feel it. Think about what was happening, who was there, what was being said, and most of all, think about what you were feeling. This is the critical part of this activity; you have to experience the feelings you felt when you had the experience initially. The more intense you can make this experience, the more you will get out of it. Now, shift to a positive memory. Again, think about what was happening, who was there, what was said, and what you were feeling. Feel it. Enjoy it. Flip back to the same or another negative memory. Go at least three times each, to a positive and a negative memory. DO THIS NOW.

You've just done what actors do all the time. I refer to this as "state manipulation." When an actor cries in a movie, he is remembering or drawing on an experience of real sadness that he has experienced so he can display genuine emotion. Now that you've experienced this and established your ability to perform state manipulation, consider what a powerful tool this is.

Sports psychologists who work with the top athletes in the world focus on this with their clients. Athletes are repeatedly forced to deal with the ups and downs of competition, and they are unable to perform at their optimum level without being in the right "state," the right frame of mind. Often during a tennis match, commentators will refer to a player's body language between points as an indication of where they are at mentally and how they can be expected to perform based on this. Is the player hunched over with a sullen look or is he moving confidently, head up and shoulders square? A smile during competition, even after losing a tough point, can be a great sign because it reflects the ability to dismiss the disappointment of losing the point and move on.

Tennis is a great sport to watch body language because the score changes after every "play" or point, and each point is followed by downtime before the serve and the next point is played. Many top players develop rituals that they follow to refocus themselves to be mentally ready for the next point, such as adjusting the strings of their racquet. They follow these rituals regardless of whether they have won or lost the previous point. You can watch a tennis player's facial expression unobstructed by a helmet or face mask for signs of frustration or confidence. Sometimes a player hits a great shot that can pull him out of a funk and reenergize his state. In team sports, sometimes one specific play, like a ferocious dunk in basketball or an interception in football, shifts the attitude of a whole team, not just the player who makes the play.

State manipulation is something you can practice at any time, especially when you are in any stressful circumstances. As soon as you feel pressure of any kind, if you look for something that can be the least bit amusing and remark about it, in spite of the circumstances, you will diffuse any building pressure. And if you can manage a smile when you are troubled, your mood will shift.

Is changing your mood as simple as holding a pencil between your teeth? The short answer is yes. How is this possible? Biting on a pencil activates "smile" muscles in your face and this has been shown to improve mood.

The mind/body connection is a two-way street. Research confirms that not only does the body respond to what the mind is thinking, but the mind responds to what the body is doing. Our posture, our body position, affects what others think and feel about us, but more importantly, it also affects how we think and feel about ourselves. If we wish to go "outside in" to affect our state, we can change our physiology. We can look up, breathe deeply, crack a smile, throw our shoulders back, and shift to a dynamic posture.

People who are depressed look depressed. When someone is ecstatic about something, you can tell by looking at them. **State presents as a phenomenon in which the old adage "Looks can be deceiving" does not generally apply. When we think of state, it's more a case of "What you see is what you get," or perhaps more specifically, "What you see (in the mirror) is what you have."** The depressed look of head down, hunched shoulders, and sullen facial expression is something anyone can recognize. A depressed state comes complete with a shallow breathing pattern.

Certain body positions are associated with power. Expressions of power include open positions, such as having your arms extended up or out. What's referred to as the "Wonder Woman" pose, hands on hips, feet apart, is another power pose. Another is standing with your hands palm down on a table in front of you as you lean on them. This places you essentially in a four-point power stance. Weak body positions are those in which you close yourself in or shrink in some way, such as hunching your shoulders, tilting your head down, or holding your neck with your hand.

Powerful leaders have high-testosterone and low-cortisol levels. (High cortisol is a sign of stress.) In an experiment rating reactions after holding a power pose for just two minutes, testers found a significant increase in testosterone levels and a significant decrease in cortisol. Two minutes of a low power or weak pose resulted in the exact opposite: a decrease in testosterone and an increase in cortisol. This is your body's chemistry talking back to you as a result of how you are standing. Those who purposely adopted a power stance also were more inclined to take risks, such as engaging in gambling. In a job interview test, those who held a power pose prior to being filmed in a job interview were judged to be more attractive candidates than those who did not. It's amazing to consider the fact that how you stand before going in to a job interview could determine whether you get the job!

Think about some other ways that you could use your body to change your mood. If you really want to break out of a funk, how about skipping? You just can't skip down the street in a cloud of doom. That would be like throwing a piece of wood in a river and expecting it to float upstream. You can confirm this principle for yourself right now. Put a genuine smile on your face. Now, try thinking of something sad while you hold a smile. DO THIS NOW.

If you keep the smile on your face during this exercise, you'll find that you can't really feel the full impact of the sadness you would otherwise be able to feel. This helps us understand how integrated our mental and physical system is. You can also do this with certain yoga poses that put you in a power position. Poses such as cobra pose and bow pose put you in a position that opens your chest dramatically by pulling your shoulders back. Warrior pose puts you in a powerful lunging position. Any of these poses would counter a gloomy, depressed state of mind.

One other thing we can use to leverage a change of state is to think about the people who count on us or rely on us. If you're a parent, a brother, sister, a friend, or a worker, then no doubt you have people who count on you in one way or another. Your relationship with these people is important and valuable. You are needed. That's a good place to be, and you can use this fact to remind yourself of your own value.

I know, at times, I've hesitated to reach out for a hand for help with even simple things because I didn't want to "owe" anybody anything, but I've come to realize what a shortsighted approach this is. **A great life is a connected life. Asking for and returning favors builds connections.** So, when I hold myself back in this way I'm really withdrawing from the richness of life. When we can use some help, we shouldn't hesitate to ask for it, and when we can give help, we should welcome the chance to do so.

You can also consider how much more helpful and how much more fun you are when you are in a positive state. Your ability to effectively serve all those people who rely on you is directly related to your state. Feeling good is better for you and everyone around you. So, why not? And since I'm sure you don't like being around people who are negative, you can assume your friends feel the same way. So, the next time you find yourself mired in a negative state, remember that you need to work to pull yourself out of it because your friends and family are counting on you.

As we look at the phenomenon of our state, we can acknowledge that our lives will be a reflection of the states that we maintain. Our state, at any given time, will determine how effective we are at anything that we choose to do, and how happy we are as we do it. It will also be the primary factor in how healthy we are and how long we live. We can choose to learn to control our state, or we can let our state shift and bounce randomly in and out of anger, depression, and frustration, while individuals and events that we do not control act and occur around us.

I'm not suggesting that all there is to do is to hold a pencil between our teeth to activate our smile muscles and everything will be fine. But the fact is everything that we've discussed here points to the fact that **if we're going to live a life of power, one in which we can freely pursue and achieve the life of our dreams, we are going to have to seize control of our state.** We are going to have to stop losing control to powerless and painful states. We need to treat our mind and our body as a trainable system, one in which we can push ourselves to maintain optimum states for wherever we are and whatever it is that we want to do. Our very lives are a daily training ground in which we can develop our personal sense of discipline.

So, we need to maintain an awareness of our state. Then, we need to use our mind to change or refocus our thoughts as necessary, and to use our body to shift ourselves into an optimum state. When challenges appear and we respond, not with frustration or fear, but with the confidence and resourcefulness that allows us to effectively deal with the circumstances, then we'll know that our training is paying off. We'll know that our state is under our control, and that's right where it should be.

○⟨⟩ POINTS TO REMEMBER: ⟨⟩○

- The beauty is nobody can exercise more control over your emotions and your moods than you can. And the payoff is massive.
- The fact is there's no such thing as a bad day. We don't live a day at a time, or an hour, or even a minute at a time. We live a moment at a time.
- State is an internal phenomenon.
- Emotional health and joy will not only bring us better days, they will bring us more of them.
- Changing state basically comes down to one of two things. You can change your thoughts or change your stance. We can go "inside out" or "outside in."
- We need to pay attention to what we pay attention to.
- The mind/body connection is a two-way street. Not only does the body respond to what the mind is thinking, but the mind responds to what the body is doing.
- State presents as a phenomenon in which the old adage "Looks can be deceiving" does not generally apply. When we think of state, it's more a case of "What you see is what you get," or perhaps more specifically, "What you see (in the mirror) is what you have."
- A great life is a connected life. Asking for and returning favors builds connections.
- If we're going to live a life of power, one in which we can freely pursue and achieve the life of our dreams, we are going to have to seize control of our state.

THE KID IDENTITY

*One of the virtues of being very young is that you don't
let the facts get in the way of your imagination.*
—Sam Levenson

*The end of childhood is when things cease to astonish us. When the world seems
familiar, when one has got used to existence, one has become an adult.*
—Eugène Ionesco

Children have neither past nor future; they enjoy the present, which very few of us do.
—Jean de La Bruyère

A man is getting old when he walks around a puddle instead of through it.
—R.C. Ferguson

My childhood may be over, but that doesn't mean playtime is.
— Ron Olson

The reluctance to put away childish things may be a requirement of genius.
—**Rebecca Pepper Sinkler**

When I grow up I want to be a little boy.
—**Joseph Heller**

Who wants to be a kid again? There are those who would love to be a kid again, and those who would never want to be a kid again, and then there are people like me. I never stopped being a kid. My inner child is more than alive and well. He's frequently on full display, like when I play with my kids.

If you continued to learn like a kid, by age forty you would know ten to twenty-five languages. If you were a girl, you would have four hundred Barbies, and if you were a boy, you would have three armored divisions with at least 1,000 toy tanks. If you continued to act like a kid, you wouldn't spend all day worrying about the mortgage, or the rent, or your retirement, or your car payment, or whether you had enough insurance. You wouldn't worry about the things your neighbors or friends have that you don't have, or the things you've always wanted but couldn't afford, all the things you feel you need in order to be able to say that you've "made it" and now you're living the life of your dreams.

If you continued to act like a kid, you wouldn't worry about these things. What would that be like? The fact is in many ways kids are better at "living" than grownups. They haven't "learned" all the grownup ways to look at things. They haven't become saddled with grownup prejudices, and stereotypes, and inhibitions, and worries. Just think about how effective, powerful, and free this makes them. Let's take a look at some winning lessons we can learn from kids.

GAL (Grow and Learn) Kids Love to Learn

Let's face it, kids are always learning and they love it. Kids are always growing. Learning is what the mind is designed to do. The more you learn, the more effective your brain is, and the more effective your brain, the better you feel and the healthier you are.

Why would we stop learning? We might as well ask why we would stop living. It was the great jurist Oliver Wendell Holmes Jr. who said, "Once the mind has been stretched by a new idea, it will never again return to its original size." In other words, just like our expanding universe, our mind can be continuously expanded by exposure to new ideas. As long as we keep learning, our minds don't get older, they get bigger. The more we can think of, the more we can comprehend, and the more we can comprehend, the more we can think of, and . . . . Being a kid and continually seeing the new is invigorating. Kids are curious. They ask why. How often do you ask why?

Kids don't worry about whether a question might make them look stupid. If they want to know, they ask. Confident people aren't afraid to ask either. In fact, in most circumstances when you ask about something, your curiosity will be appreciated more than your silence. Two good things happen when you ask questions. You learn something and expand your mind, and you give someone a chance to enjoy sharing their knowledge.

This is a good time to revisit the concept of self-talk in a way that relates to kids. Think about what we do when we are working to help a child learn something new. There's a general rule to follow whether a child is learning to walk, to ride a bike, jump rope, read, write, or do arithmetic. We might call it high-frequency repetitive reinforcement (HFRR).

A child is learning to walk and each time they get up, down they go, as they work to establish their balance. Walking and bike riding are balance activities, and there is generally a lot of falling and failure as part of the learning curve. But we don't laugh at the child who falls, and we don't berate them. What do we do? We cheer them on. We cheer each successive failure with enthusiastic words of encouragement. "That's it, Tommy, that's it! You almost stood on your own that time. You can do it!" These statements are made over and over again for as long as it takes Tommy to walk because we want Tommy to keep trying, and we know that he's going to walk sooner or later.

I've been working on teaching my son to read the same way I taught his sister. My practice is to enthusiastically praise him every other minute or so even if he misses a word we've been over fifty times. After all, he just turned five, and if I bark at him or ridicule him, then getting him to sit down and read is going to become a nightly battle. He'll resent our reading lessons whether he's improving or not. And my task to develop his ability will be infinitely harder.

Constant encouragement is key. Why can't our self-talk about our own efforts take the same approach? They can. They should. After all, in one sense, there's never any real failure at anything until you throw in the towel and give up. Until then, all the missteps are just part of the learning curve. This is a great reason not to beat ourselves up every time something didn't work out the way we wanted it to.

Let's take someone who's working to lose weight. Perhaps they've been working at this for some time without success because they haven't been able to stick with a program. They might start to doubt their ability to succeed at all. They might start to tell themselves that they just don't have the ability to lose weight. That couldn't be true but they might start to feel like it is. The laws of physics tell us that if you consume less calories than you burn on a daily basis, then your body will have to burn off reserves, causing you to lose weight. This is an established fact, a straightforward rule. All you have to do is follow it.

The diet industry is made up of an infinite number of ways to comply with this basic law of physics. People can jump from diet to diet or work with one diet long-term without success, but their lack of success means they're simply not meeting the basic rule of consuming less calories than they burn. The hunt for the "right" diet is not a diet that changes the basic rule; it's simply an effort by an individual to find the easiest way to apply the basic rule. When people doubt their ability to succeed in losing weight, we know it's not because they believe the laws of physics don't apply to them, rather they doubt their ability to do what they must: to consistently consume less then they burn.

So, what's to be done? Treat yourself like a kid. Encourage yourself like a kid. Don't beat yourself up because you haven't lost weight yet. Think of yourself like a kid who's learning to walk or learning to read. You haven't actually been "dieting" yet, you've merely been "training" to go on a diet. You've been intermittently practicing the skill you need to go on a diet. Some days you've consumed less than you've burned and some days you haven't, just like a kid learning to read who gets some words right and some words wrong. When a child consistently gets enough words right, we say they can read. When you consistently consume less than you burn, you'll lose weight. So each time you eat a sensible meal and don't overindulge, give yourself that enthusiastic slap on the back. Say something like what I tell my son: "Wow, Evan, you just read the word 'snowball.' You never read that word by yourself before. That was awesome!" You can tell yourself, "Wow, you just ate a chicken salad with one tablespoon of low-cal dressing. That's exactly what you need to do. That's it!"

Getting back to the idea of learning, sometimes kids don't need all of that encouragement to learn because they already want to know something. Reading is a major skill that takes time, patience, and discipline to develop, but kids genuinely love to learn to do new things and to know more. Learn like a kid. While there are a lot of great things about acting like a kid, this is the greatest.

PTB (Pretend to Be) Kids Love Make Believe

Pretending is one of the great underappreciated skills in this world. Underappreciated by adults, but not by kids. Kids can be anybody they want to be. They are natural actors with an ability to adapt to any role that they want to play. They don't need a script, a director, a film crew, an acting coach, costumes, or props . . . though having a few toys doesn't hurt. They can be a fireman, spaceman, policeman, soldier, teacher, fashion designer, race car driver, or deep sea diver. They can be all of these things in a single day. As a knight, they can slay a dragon. How many of us have the ability to slay a dragon? Without the heart of a kid and the ability to pretend, that's a fairly daunting task.

Why let pretending become the lost art of our childhood? This is a skill that can pay serious dividends in any endeavor. A kid giving a speech can be John F. Kennedy, Winston Churchill, or Martin Luther King Jr. He can inspire a country, offer blood, toil, tears, and sweat, or have a dream. He can win the Daytona and Indianapolis 500s, the Kentucky Derby and the Triple Crown, the World Cup and the Stanley Cup. A kid can be a fashion model on Broadway, a pop star in London, or a national news anchor on television. Kids can go anywhere and be anybody they choose in their heads. And that's the whole point of identity design.

You decide who you are. You decide how brave you are, how dedicated you are, how disciplined you are. You can pretend to be your favorite role models, from Hollywood or the real world, whenever you choose. While we may not need to slay dragons, literally, we all have our own dragons to slay. If we were kids, we would pretend we could do whatever it is we have to do. As adults, we can do the same.

I can remember reestablishing my connection with being another character as an adult when I took some acting classes. My instructor was fairly intense, and I performed in some one-act plays and I found it to be all-consuming. When I went to movies at this time, especially intense dramas and thrillers, which I love, I found myself taking on the feelings of the lead character. As he was faced with a dangerous situation, I would feel my pulse quicken as I thought about what I was going to do and how I was going to do it. This made going to the movies not simply a form of escapism but a full-blown, adrenaline-fueled adventure. It was a very different experience and just recalling and writing about it here reminds me that I need to reconnect with this.

Now, with or without a specific "task," think of one of your favorite characters from films, books, or the real world and pretend to be that character for at least two minutes. Walk like him (or her), talk like him, and be him in every way, just like you pretended to be somebody as a kid. DO THIS NOW.

Hopefully you fully enjoyed this little activity. You can do this whenever you like, and in order to enjoy the benefits of this, you don't even have to be good at it. Remember, you're only "pretending." Kids can slip in and out of pretend mode so easily that we don't think of it as anything special at all. So, give yourself the freedom to do this often. Even if it's only briefly, pretend or think of yourself as another character. Do this at least once a day for the next two weeks. Then, when you really need it, you've got it.

TFR (Tolerability Failure Rate) Kids Aren't Afraid to Fall Down

Kids have a high tolerance for the "F" word, "failure." In the first years of life, they don't even know the word or what it means. It's part of their resilience and one of their primary learning skills. Think of a child learning to walk. What's the first thing you see them do? Fall down. And the next thing you see them do? Fall down. And the next? Has anyone ever counted how many times a child falls down in the process of learning to walk? No matter what that number is, kids are oblivious to it because they're not focused on how many times they fall down. They just want to walk. They don't see falling down as failure. It's not part of their vocabulary. When my son is learning something new that involves balance, he says things like "Look, Papa, did you see me fall?" as if his fall were only intended for my entertainment.

When kids conquer something new, something they've really worked at, their sense of accomplishment is palpable. I'll never forget the first time my daughter, Michelle, climbed up on our yellow-leather living room couch all by herself. She had been working at this for a while and this time seemed particularly determined to do it. As soon as she got up on the seat cushion, she spun around and flashed a look of triumph equivalent to one athletes give for achieving a gold medal. A photograph capturing that moment would be among my most prized possessions. She not only learned how to get up on the couch, she realized that by applying herself she could learn how to do something that was initially beyond her reach. Priceless (the look and the lesson).

What's your tolerability failure rate? How many times will you attempt something before you give up? We make such a big deal out of failure. Why? This is a completely learned response. As a learned response, it's a lesson we could do without. Think about a time when you didn't even know the word or what it meant. Feel how liberating it is not to know what failure is. Think like a kid. Act like a kid. Fall down. Get up. Fall down. Get up. Keep going. And when you get there, don't be shy about acknowledging what you've done. The world loves a winning smile, especially when there's an understanding of the effort that went into earning it when it didn't come easy.

PWA (Play with Anybody) Kids Like All Kinds of Kids

Watch kids at a playground. They're like human magnets as they make new friends, running and jumping and sliding and swinging together. They don't have any preconceptions about who should or shouldn't be their friend. They come to a playground to play, and they'd rather play with others than by themselves. Their attitude seems to be two's company and three or more are a party. Fun is especially contagious for kids. If one kid seems to be having a particularly good time, others will want a piece of the action. The fact that they may not have seen each other before, and that they may not look much like each other, is irrelevant. Fun is fun.

I recently signed up my five-year-old son for a baseball team. As it turns out, Evan was the only white kid on an otherwise all-black team. When he went to his first game, he immediately started kidding around with the kid next to him on the bench. They were going head-to-head, pushing each other with the visors on their baseball hats. It was the kind of simple goofy playing around that kids do. They had never met before, and they were having fun. Can you imagine two adults meeting and engaging with each other in this way? As an adult, if someone did that to you, your first reaction would likely be to tell them to get out of your face. But as kids, my son and his teammate were kidding around. There was nothing to worry about; there was nothing to do but have fun. This is the way it is for kids.

As adults, we are so much more guarded when it comes to making new friends, even on a casual basis. Why is this? (Look at that, just like a kid, I'm not afraid to ask why!) What exactly are we guarding? While there may be reason to use caution in certain situations, in general, as grownups, we can do a much better job of connecting like kids do. Research tells us that the more connected we are, the healthier and happier we are, so here again, acting like a kid will pay real dividends. The fact that kids are so accepting of others is a healthy and joyful way to be.

Some things you can do to put yourself in a position to make new friends include signing up for a class in an area of personal interest, going on a trip with an organized group, or volunteering in some community effort. These activities provide chances to learn, to enjoy, or to serve while you develop new connections. The next time you find yourself in a setting where you don't know most of the people there, you can think of yourself as a kid at the playground, free to smile and say hello, to initiate contact with anyone—just like real kids do.

ITM (In the Moment) Kids Believe in NOW

A kid's clock is always set to the same time: now. If kids are doing something they like doing, they don't want to stop, and if they're doing something they don't like, they want to stop now. If they want to do something, saying that they can do it next week or tomorrow, or even an hour from now, is like saying they can't do it at all.

Of course, we can't always do whatever we want, whenever we want, but this characteristic is a good reflection on how much "now" means to kids, and how much they live in the moment. While it may be easy for us to say kids don't have as much to think about as adults do, that they don't have as much to worry about, the fact is being in the moment is a powerful way to be. Not only do they live in the moment, kids tend to run on "one-thing-at-a-time" software, which research tells us is the most efficient way to operate.

Multitasking has been referred to as doing two or more things at once, such as listening to music and reading, switching back and forth between tasks, or performing a number of tasks in rapid succession. Research indicates that there is a loss in efficiency as a result of multitasking.

In *Psychology Today*, Kendra Cherry reports on the research of Joshua Rubinstein, Jeffrey Evans, and David Meyer. (See Kendra Cherry. "Multitasking, The Cognitive Costs of Multitasking." Psychology.About.com.) They found that individuals lost significant amounts of time as they switched between multiple tasks. As tasks became more complex, individuals lost even more time. The researchers reported two stages involved in the executive control process that governs switching tasks in the brain.

They refer to the first stage as "goal shifting," the process of deciding to do one task instead of another. The second stage is "role activation," changing from the rules of one task to the rules of another. It's understandable that the more time we spend deciding what to do and changing from one thing to another, the less time we spend performing the tasks we want to do.

An exception to the problem of multitasking can be made when the two tasks are learned tasks that don't require much brainpower. You can walk and chew gum at the same time. In fact, you can walk and do a lot of things without too much trouble. However, the other day I was thinking about a segment in this book and became so wrapped up in my thoughts that I started to walk through a traffic light into oncoming traffic. Fortunately, I survived. I am writing about this after all. I don't recall this happening to me before. It seems that for some of us even walking and thinking can be a dangerous combination.

Let's look at one particularly damaging bit of multitasking. Watching television and eating are a bad combination. Watching television focuses your attention on what you are watching and distracts you from what you are eating. We tend to eat faster and to eat more when we are watching because we're not paying attention to what we're eating. The more you are distracted, the more likely you are to eat more. For years, I used to tell myself that I could concentrate on my food and whatever I wanted to watch on television at the same time. Now I know this is simply not true. Why not eliminate the distraction of the television altogether by not turning it on?

We have no control over the past. What's done is done. We can do things that will surely influence the future, but our control there is limited. There are so many variables that come into play as time moves forward. Being in the moment is a naturally more powerful and joyful way to be. It's the place we can exercise our greatest measure of control. And as we've already noted, control is power that we can use to shape the life of our dreams. Being in the moment, living in the now, means just that, not tonight, not in an hour, nor in a minute, but now. So, why not act like a kid and focus our attention where it matters most—NOW.

PDPH (Play Deep Play Hard) Kids Like to Bring the Heat

When kids play, they don't just play around. They get serious. They throw themselves into what they are doing. They bring a full-bodied approach to play that's exhilarating to watch. Sometimes the best thing about watching my son play is just listening to the soundtrack he generates. He'll be talking or making noises that perfectly match whatever he's doing. It's awesome. It's a reflection of how completely he's engaged in whatever he's playing. This is a reflection of the natural inclination of kids to find a state of flow. At what point did we stop creating a soundtrack to go with our activities?

Do we bring a kid's enthusiasm to the things that we do, to anything that we do? The quality of our lives is driven by the energy we generate. We get back what we put in, we give to receive, and we live as we give. We cannot very well expect the life of our dreams to show up in return for a mediocre effort on our part.

While it's true we have to work smart to get what we want, both "work" and "smart" are the operative words here. We need to play hard, and work hard too. We need to bring some of that childlike intensity to the things we do. We may not need to generate the surround-sound soundtrack that kids do, but we can model their overall commitment to what they're doing. We can act like a kid and play deep and hard.

TOSN (Take on Something New) Kids Like Doing Things They've Never Done Before

Taking up new things is a natural for kids. For many grownups, the battle cry seems to be "Just make it through another day." Surviving is not living. It's surviving. For kids, the world is not something to be survived; it's something to be discovered. This means when they see something new, they want to give it a whirl. But as adults, how many of us are looking for something new to do? I'm not suggesting we all have to go skydiving tomorrow, but taking on something new is a sure way to push the envelope and get us out of our comfort zone. Let's remind ourselves of what Oliver Wendell Holmes said about stretching the mind. Taking on new things is a subset of learning and growing, and it deserves special attention because it leads to its own experiential learning.

A few years ago my brother Mike started telling me about these surf camps in Costa Rica that he found on the Internet where gringos like us who grew up in the rustbelt in places like Michigan, a good thousand miles from any decent surf, were learning to catch waves. At first this sounded a little crazy to me. Mike had always been a big fan of surfing and surf music, and he was talking about these camps as if he were serious about actually going to one. Mike doesn't always think like a kid. Sometimes he thinks like a teenager.

I started to think about it, and it occurred to me that if these camps were actually surviving, from a business standpoint, people must be going to these places and they must be actually learning how to surf. Otherwise, the word would get out that this was some sort of bogus fantasy pipe-dream and business would dry up like a wet noodle in the desert. Not wanting to miss out on a big adventure, once I began thinking this could actually work, I gave Mike the green light on the surf dog road trip, and it turned out to be a blast. The beaches, the sunsets, the food, the people, and the surf all made for a gringo getaway that I'll never forget.

Don't get me wrong, it was a lot of work getting out in the surf just to get into position to try to catch a wave. It definitely takes you out of your comfort zone, and you need a fairly high tolerability failure rate, as discussed above. The wipeouts you pull while climbing the learning curve are like putting your head through a car wash. When I got back to the States, I was draining out for days. It seemed like my head had developed a cluster of compartments for all the water I had taken in, and they were on some kind of intermittent delayed drainage schedule. But the bottom line is catching waves on a surfboard is an organic experience that I'll never forget, something I would have missed if I didn't act like a kid!

FBC (Full Body Contact) Kids Dig Contact

Research tells us how important human touch is to our well-being. Kids revel in touch, from grabbing and squeezing to hugging and wrestling and free-for-all horseplay. They seem to have an innate understanding that our bodies were intended to be in contact. They know that it feels good to feel. Watching kids in unstructured play can sometimes look like an informal wrestling match. Compare this with the level of touch we experience as adults. Some adults may go days without much more physical contact than a handshake. While this might be considered "normal," is it healthy?

Unfortunately, if you're not a kid, you may well be touch deprived. Touch deprivation has been referred to as "skin hunger" and increases stress and body tension. In her article "Bridging the Great Divide: Touching Our Most Basic Humanity," http:HealingHeartPower.com/article1.html, Linda Marks points out that a lack of touch can cause sleep disturbances and lowered immune response, which results in greater vulnerability to illness. Emotional, physical, and cognitive development are all impaired by a lack of touch.

The anthropologist Margaret Mead cited a correlation between levels of touch and aggression. Cultures in which individuals experience frequent touch are more peaceful than cultures that minimize physical contact. She studied the Mundugumor people in Papua New Guinea, who have a practice of carrying infants in a basket, out of contact with the mother's body. They are a generally aggressive and warlike people. And Romanian orphans deprived of touch fail to develop physically, emotionally, and intellectually. Bad things happen when people don't experience touch on a regular basis.

Studies have shown the elderly enjoy greater health when they experience regular touch. Psychologist Matthew Hertenstein, PhD, director of the Touch and Emotion Lab at DePauw University, reports that human touch has been shown to lower blood pressure and cortisol levels, which reduces stress. A hug or pat on the back, even a friendly handshake, send a message to our central nervous system, which can induce a feeling of happiness and joy according to neurologist Shekar Raman, MD. It doesn't matter if you are touching someone or being touched. Dr. Raman reports that the more positive physical contact you have with others, even at a minimal level, the happier you'll be.

In an article for *The Huffington Post*, "The Power of Touch: How Physical Contact Can Improve Your Health," <http:huffingtonpost.com/2013/05/14/the-power-of-touch-physical-contact-health_n_3253987.html>, Diana Spechler makes a good case for focusing on touch in a way that makes each instance an opportunity for a mutual gift. Just reaching out for contact creates a chance to do something good for yourself and someone else, at no more cost than the thought to do so. If kids can do it, we can too.

FOM (Freedom of Movement) Kids Believe in Motion

Kids move. Kids stretch. Moving is good for the body and good for the mind. No big revelation here. The health risks of being a couch potato are well documented. I don't know any kids who I would characterize as couch potatoes. They're more like Energizer bunnies. They run, jump, skip, hop, roll, flip, and swing with abandon. They ramble, and scramble, and tumble, and twirl. They shimmy and shake. As with touch, kids know that our bodies were meant to move, to move freely. We were designed with arms and legs, and hands and feet, and more than 600 muscles to move every part of our body every which way. Kids use them more and in more ways than grownups. They can't help it. They're kinetic.

As for stretching, kids are naturally limber and enjoy the feel of a real stretch. Stretching is a vastly overlooked part of our fitness regimen as adults. However, the rising popularity of yoga is introducing intense stretching to more people every day. I started practicing yoga over ten years ago, and my practice has truly been a blessing. When I started, my hamstrings were tighter than high-octave piano strings. After yoga workouts, I would literally feel the backs of my legs tingle from stimulation for the rest of the day. It was a great feeling, and I've regained real flexibility in my legs and body. I have a few yoga poses that I do every day.

Yoga works the mind as well. Spontaneous insights are part of the experience of yoga as you work within yourself. Stretching reduces stress and increases circulation as well as flexibility and range of motion. As we age, our muscles tend to become shorter and tighter, and stretching is the antidote. Without stretching, the loss of range of motion can become crippling. We have all seen an elderly person whose stride has been reduced to baby steps due to a loss of range of motion. Not a pretty sight.

I've had numerous injuries over the years that have restricted my movement in various ways. At times, movements as simple as walking and climbing stairs were a chore. At one point, due to pain I had in my lower back, I was only able to take steps deliberately, one step at a time. Each time I went up the stairs, I was reminded of my limitation. Thankfully, as I write this, I have recovered from my most recent challenges and am basically free to do as I choose.

I lived in a one-story home for approximately fourteen years. When I moved into my current two-story home, I realized how much I had missed having stairs at home. I make it a regular practice to bound up stairs two at a time, which serves as a reminder of a time when such an action would have been impossible. Now when I climb the stairs, it feels like a cross between jumping, gliding, and flying, and it triggers my deep sense of gratitude that I have the ability to do it. Every time I go up the stairs, I assert my power. Stairs are a silent affirmation. I don't look at stairs as something to be tolerated. Stairs are a runway, an invitation to fly. I take on stairs the same way I did as a kid.

Dancing is practiced in cultures all over the world. It's a way to connect your mind, body, and soul. It's a way to express yourself. It's a way to feel rhythm. Kids are enthusiastic dancers, and there's no reason for us not to dance when we get the chance. You don't need a partner or to go to a club. You can turn on some music and just dance.

We all have movements we remember that we associate with our childhood. Think of skipping. When was the last time you skipped? (I'm not talking about skipping school! Or work!) I was skipping the other day with my kids. They wanted to skip to Blake's house, down the block. It's the kind of movement that makes you years younger just doing it. You can't help but laugh at yourself as you repeat this basic movement from childhood. Think of other movements that take you back in this way, such as somersaults, rolling down a hill, making angels in the snow, spinning, or "skinning the cat" on a bar. What about shimmying? When is the last time you shimmied? Dust off these old favorites and see how you feel, because when you move like a kid, you feel like a kid.

LED (Laugh Every Day) Kids Have a Very Active Funny Bone

Is there any better way to experience fun than having a good laugh? Ha, ha. I said is there any better way? Kids are like gurgling fountains bubbling with laughter. And the benefits of laughter? The *New York Tribune* reports, "A good, real, unrestrained, hearty laugh is a sort of glorified internal massage, performed rapidly and automatically. It manipulates and revitalizes corners and unexplored crannies of the system that are unresponsive to most other exercise methods." It's undeniable that laughter is pure fun. Kids have ready access to the wholehearted kind of laughter that can serve as an emotional makeover. A deep laugh is all encompassing and leaves no room for simultaneous worry or misery.

It's easy to think about the link kids have with laughter. After all, kids are just playing, aren't they? But then, that's the point. Kids are playing. We could do better too, by not taking things too seriously. We could do better by not taking ourselves too seriously. A playful attitude cannot only lead to more laughs, we can also be more effective by being more relaxed and less stressed.

Take a day and approach it with the attitude that you are just going to play. If you have work to do, you will still do the work that you have to do, but do it with the attitude that you're not really working. You're just playing. See if this "approach" can put you in a more relaxed, productive state. See if you can be more effective just by playing.

I recall when Evan had to go in for some vaccination shots. My wife agonized over how our then-four-year-old son was going to deal with the pain. For the week before the appointment it was troubling her, and, to make things up to him after the ordeal was over, she planned to take him on a trip for ice cream. When I returned from work that day, the first thing I wanted to know was how Evan managed at the doctor's office, so I asked him about it. He smiled as he looked at me and said, "They just pinched me." Apparently, Evan didn't take the doctor's visit as seriously as his mother did. Apparently, when he went to the doctor's office, he was just playing and the doctor just pinched him.

• • • • •

Watching kids play can be amazing. That is, if you don't have to pick up after them. There's so much to learn from them. There is an underlying theme here to the points we've covered as we look at learning from kids and emulating kids. There is a sweet spot in the lives of kids when they've developed enough to think and do, to learn and play, but before they begin to adopt the limitations of being a "grownup." Before certain learned responses start to take hold, such as worrying about failure or how others see us. Before we start to experience what peer pressure is. Before we start consciously "conforming" to the way we believe we are supposed to act. Before we start to recognize what's "expected," and start behaving in a way that we only deliver what's expected. Unfortunately, there is evidence that kids are growing up faster and faster these days, and to the extent that this is true, this "sweet spot" that we are talking about, where kids act with carefree abandon, is shrinking.

We've looked at some of the best things about being a kid, and we can reclaim our freedom, regardless of our age or our circumstances, to reconnect with some of the attitudes that come with being a kid. It comes down to our choices. All those words and phrases like "what's expected of you," and "that's not what you're supposed to do at your age," and "conformity" don't really apply to you unless you choose to allow them to. *Identity Design* says those are other people's words and other people's thoughts. If you want to hang on to the best parts of being a kid, you have the right and the choice to do just that. Not only are you free to act like a kid, you have good reason to do so.

○⊂⊃ POINTS TO REMEMBER: ⊂⊃○

- GAL (Grow and Learn) Kids love to learn.
- PTB (Pretend to Be) Kids love make believe.
- TFR (Tolerability Failure Rate) Kids aren't afraid to fall down.
- PWA (Play with Anybody) Kids like all kinds of kids.
- ITM (In the Moment) Kids believe in NOW.
- PDPH (Play Deep Play Hard) Kids like to bring the heat.
- TOSN (Take on Something New) Kids like doing things they've never done before.
- FBC (Full Body Contact) Kids dig contact.
- FOM (Freedom of Movement) Kids believe in motion.
- LED (Laugh Every Day) Kids have a very active funny bone.

THE SERVICE IDENTITY

Act as if what you do makes a difference. It does.
—William James

*Everybody can be great, because everybody can serve. You don't
have to have a college degree . . . you only need a heart full of grace.*
—Martin Luther King Jr. (paraphrased)

*I slept and I dreamed that life is all joy. I woke and I saw that
life is all service. I served and I saw that service is joy.*
—Attributed to **Kahlil Gibran**

Never decide to do nothing just because you can only do little.
—Steve Maraboli

You make a living by what you earn and a life by what you give.
—Frequently attributed to ***Winston Churchill***

Love must be as much a light as it is a flame.
—Henry David Thoreau

Are you in service? Who and how and why do you serve? Service is the ultimate action for personal fulfillment. Research shows serving affirms our connection with others, builds our self-esteem by establishing our value, and makes our hearts grow stronger. We become healthier and happier when we serve, when we give, when we love. The more we give, the more of us there is to give. If you want to make a friend, change the world, and feel alive, serve somebody.

If you're not giving, you're not connecting. It's as simple as that. No man is an island. No woman is a stone. You cannot expect to feel fulfilled or happy alone. If you feel alone, the quickest remedy is not to strategize how you are going to develop relationships or get people to like you. The quickest remedy is to do something for someone. The more of yourself you give to others, the more of you there is to give. Think of how you appreciate others who have been kind to you. You build confidence and a sense of your own inherent value and worth when you give.

We don't take our possessions with us when we're gone. We think we "own" our possessions, but in fact, we're only renting these things until we're gone. **The only thing that matters when we're gone, the only thing that counts, is what we've done for others.** After this, everything else is irrelevant. A life designed only for your own benefit will ring hollow by every measure. None of us live in a vacuum. The fact is selfishness is useless. It's a distraction. There's no such thing as a happy selfish person.

At a subatomic level, we are all connected in a swirl of space. Quantum physics tells us that, at our most basic level, we are nothing more than energy and information interconnected in a vast cosmic soup. We need to appreciate this connection. It's one of the reasons that injustice to one is injustice to all. We cannot tolerate behavior that belittles or demeans anyone. There's no place for it. Unfortunately, there's injustice all around us. But the more enlightened we become, the less there will be. As we commit more deeply to serving each other, we will naturally reduce the injustice in the world.

The forces of greed, and materialism, and selfishness divide us. Every step we take that moves us away from others adds to the alienation in this world and fosters more injustice. Service reverses this phenomenon. Most of us can recall experiences where we found ourselves truly giving of ourselves to others. It might have been under circumstances where a family member was injured or in need of help. It may have been a situation where there was a breakdown of some sort, such as a power outage or a damaging storm, and our help was needed.

There's a certain clarity that emerges when someone who you are with is in deep need of your help, because you realize that for the moment that you need to provide that help, nothing else matters. You are not distracted because you realize that, under the circumstances, anything that might normally distract you is irrelevant. If you think of these experiences, I'm sure you can recall the beauty of the feeling of helping others. It's a universal feeling. Each time there is some overwhelming disaster, we see examples of people pulling together in extraordinary ways in response to the common need to address the hardships caused by a hurricane, a tsunami, a terrorist attack, or some other event.

These events are touchstones for our connectedness. New York residents recall that in the days following 9/11, the normal boundaries and class divisions disappeared. People greeted each other on the street and were more considerate and sensitive to each other. Was this a taste of heaven on earth? This was a response to a tragic event and an extremely stressful set of circumstances. Studies suggest that acute stress may lead to greater cooperative and friendly behavior. In *Scientific American*, Emma Seppälä said she believes this group response may be responsible for our collective survival as a species. Researchers have found that after acute stress, men became more trusting of others and were more likely to cooperate with others as they played an economic game based on joint efforts.

Decades of research show that social connection is a basic human need, and it has been linked to psychological and physical health, including a stronger immune system, faster recovery from disease, and even longevity. **The quality of our lives is a function of the quality of our relationships. And there is no better way to build our relationships than to give.** Love is the ultimate gift, and as that quote from Henry David Thoreau indicates, it must be a light, a light which illuminates us. "Love must be as much a light as it is a flame."

A student once asked renowned anthropologist Margaret Mead about the first sign of civilization in a given culture. Expecting the response to be a clay pot or a primitive tool of some kind, he was surprised to hear her answer, "A healed femur."

Mead explained that no healed femurs could be found where the law of the jungle, the survival of the fittest, operated. The healed femur was a sign that someone cared. A sign that someone did the hunting and gathering for the injured person until their leg could heal. This evidence of compassion, according to Mead, is the first sign of civilization.

Take a moment to think of where we would be if we had continued to live strictly by the law of the jungle, if we were driven only by the credo of every man for himself. The marvels of modern day society, of man's scientific progress, would never be possible. For as many evils that persist today, you would have to acknowledge we've come an incredibly long way from our humble beginnings as a race of simple hunters and gatherers. So, if the first sign of compassion is the first sign of civilization, we can't escape the fact that we need that compassion to play a central role in our lives.

Psychologists Les Parrott and Neil Clark Warren suggest that compassion and self-giving love also serve as the first sign of personal fulfillment. They suggest the ability to serve self-giving love without seeking a return is the "hinge" upon which a happy life hangs, that you can't be happy without love no matter what wealth, or power, or honors you possess. They define the term "self-giving love" as selfishness in reverse, as love that is not concerned with benefits and expects nothing in return.

Love and giving lead us to practice empathy. Love and empathy feed each other. Empathy is the practice of understanding and experiencing the feelings, thoughts, and experience of another. Studies show this quality, more than any other, to be at the very heart of loving others. Empathy is a deep way to connect with a friend because you're not only listening to them, you're working to put yourself in their shoes.

The more grateful you are, the more loving and giving you become. Here's an activity that increases your gratitude and your giving at the same time. Identify key people in your life, and make a list of things you appreciate about each person. When you are with a particular person, think of your list and tell the person what you appreciate about them. It's great to just slip this into the conversation. For example, you mention a film you just saw and the fact that the main character was extremely loyal. You could add, "That character was almost as loyal as you are!" It helps to start with a list. So, think of some of the main people in your life and list the things that you appreciate about them. DO THIS NOW.

You now have a list that will give you the chance to express your appreciation for the good things that your friends and family bring to your life. Start sharing these thoughts with them and watch them light up as you do. You'll both feel the glow from this exchange.

Are we hardwired to give? What does it mean "to give to receive"? In an article on the benefits of giving, Jason Marsh and Jill Suttie cite a number of studies on the benefits of giving. A 2008 study by a Harvard Business School professor, Michael Norton, and colleagues found that giving money to someone else gave participants greater happiness than spending it on themselves.

In a 2006 study, Jorge Moll and colleagues at the National Institutes of Health found that when people give to charities, regions of the brain associated with pleasure, social connection, and trust were activated, creating a "warm glow" effect. Some scientists have cited giving as a trigger for the release of endorphins (our feel good chemicals) in the brain, producing a "helper's high," similar to the way running triggers the "runner's high."

Doug Oman, of the University of California, Berkeley, led a 1999 study that found that elderly people who volunteered for two or more organizations were 44 percent less likely to die over a five-year period than were nonvolunteers, even after controlling for other factors such as their age, exercise habits, general health, and negative health habits like smoking. Stephanie Brown of the University of Michigan conducted a 2003 study that produced similar results. It also found no link between receiving help and a reduced risk of death.

These studies point to the data-driven conclusion that it really is better to give than to receive. We actually do get healthier when we help others than when they help us. In a 2006 study, by Rachel Piferi of Johns Hopkins University and Kathleen Lawler of the University of Tennessee, people who provided social support to others had lower blood pressure than participants who didn't. Thus, they were able to document a link of a direct physiological benefit to those who help others.

What about the heart? Sylvia Ann Hewlett reports in *Forbes* magazine that research by the Corporation for National and Community Service reveals that **charitable work literally makes the heart grow stronger.** Individuals with coronary artery disease who participate in volunteer activities after a heart attack report a reduction in despair and depression. This drives down mortality. It adds years to life. Also, those who volunteer have fewer incidents of heart disease in the first place. And older adults who volunteered on a weekly basis showed significant gains in physical performance, such as gains in walking speed and improved cognitive function, according to Orly Avitzur in *Consumer Reports*.

Why does giving feel so good? The giver creates something good for someone by giving. This leads to two things that carry significant impact. First, the giver experiences a feeling of gratitude, not just for the fact that he did something for someone else, but that he had the ability to do so, thus reinforcing the power of his own identity. In addition, these feelings are amplified by any additional ripple effect from what the giver has done. Second, giving builds social connections. We feel closer to those who we help and they feel closer to us.

Virtually all the major religions of the world teach the principle of giving. Jesus Christ told us, "It is more blessed to give than to receive." Acts 20:35. And 2 Corinthians 9:7 tells us of God's love for a cheerful giver, reminding us that all the benefits we've discussed above, from the physical to the mental, are really only available to those who are happy to give.

In Buddhism, generosity is the first of the ten virtues an individual must attain in order to reach enlightenment. Buddha states that you can only lose what you cling to. In Islam, giving to the needy is the third of the five pillars required of a Muslim to enter paradise. The Quran speaks of giving to relatives, the needy, the poor, and the traveling alien. In Hinduism, charitable acts aid a person in their quest for nirvana, a state of release and freedom from suffering.

There is a beautiful Hindu proverb that epitomizes everything we are looking at in this discussion of the service identity. **"They who give have all things; they who withhold have nothing."** This sentiment is mirrored in the words of Lao Tzu, who said, "He who obtains has little. He who scatters has much." These are a few among the many quotations from among the greatest spiritual movements of the world laying down the word on giving. Can we choose to ignore this collective wisdom?

In researching this topic, I came across a very curious quote about giving from the eastern sage, Confucius, and I include it here for comic relief, and, no, I didn't make this up. Confucius says, "Never give a sword to a man who can't dance." A strange piece of wisdom about giving that we ignore at our own peril.

Service projects for troubled youth have been found to teach pro-social values to self-centered, anti-social, young people. These projects in which young people serve genuine human needs connect them to a new way of being. Many of these individuals have been deprived of positive personal relationships, and when they serve others, such as seniors who face the same problems, the role reversal can be enlightening. This kind of action, this role reversal, can serve as a catalyst for a deeper identity reversal. In juvenile court, when young people guilty of serious crimes reshape their identity and begin to see their own value and purpose, they begin to see the value in treating others as they want to be treated. As we look for activities that can reshape ourselves, we can do no better than to look for paths to service.

Derek Lin is a writer who has written a series of books on the Tao, the Chinese concept signifying the "way" or "path." The Tao is not a "name" or a "thing," but the underlying natural order of the universe. In Taoism, the spiritual objective is to harmonize with nature to achieve "effortless action." The Tao teaches that you already have everything you need, that you don't need to wait for or "get" something in order to be happy. In an article, "The Tao of Giving," Lin suggests some simple gifts that anyone can give:

1. The gift of a smile. A smile can be given freely to brighten someone's day.
2. The gift of connection. Maintain eye contact when you speak with others, listen intently, and stay in the moment.
3. The gift of kindness. Express thanks, encouragement, and praise to others. Think of how it makes you feel when you hear these types of things said to you. There's value here.
4. The gift of assistance. An offer to help someone or to volunteer in the community makes a difference.
5. The gift of empathy. Put yourself in someone's shoes. Recognize the importance to others of simply being understood.
6. The gift of time. Spend quality time rather than money on friends and family. Focus on others, and be in the "giving" mode during this time. This is a gift that builds memories for you and your friends.

If you look at the collective cost of these actions, you can see they add up to zero. But the benefits are priceless. Priceless! For our next activity, we select a day of the week to focus on our giving. No money needs to be given. Let me repeat, no money. A focus on the simple activities above is all that's required. Make a copy of these six giving points and review it in the morning of the day you select. I might suggest you choose Monday if that's a day you have issues with. Why not apply some reverse psychology and make it the best day of the week. According to the Tao, **you already have an unlimited supply of the greatest gifts to give to others.** Why would you leave them in the closet? What are you waiting for?

In the Sunday Style section of the *New York Times*, in a discussion of marriages and their backstory, Alice Charney Epstein explained that she had a simple test when she was in the dating scene. From the moment she met someone, she timed how long it would take until they asked her a question with the word "you" in it. Apparently, the good Mr. Epstein aced the test. How would you fare in a test like this? When you meet someone, do you immediately start talking about yourself, or do you ask the person to tell you about themselves? Whatever you've done in the past, this is a very simple fix. Simply resolve to ask someone something about themselves at the first opportunity when you meet someone new. Decide that you are going to "give" them a chance to let you get to know them.

An article in the *Harvard Business Review* titled "The Human Moment at Work" discussed how to make real contact with a person at work. It stated that the fundamental thing you have to do is turn off your cell phone, close your laptop, end your daydream, and pay full attention to the person. Sounds simple, doesn't it? Yet, how many times do you let phone calls interrupt someone when they're talking to you? How do you feel when that happens to you? There is a newly coined term for the moment when someone interrupts a conversation with you to answer their cell phone and acts as if you don't exist. The word is "pizzled," which is a combination of puzzled and pissed off. Wouldn't it be better, when you received a call which you had to answer, if you said, "Could you please excuse me? I've been expecting a call about . . .," and if you answered the phone by saying, "I'm here with John, and I just have a minute, but I can call you back later."

Guy Kawasaki has written a book called *Enchantment,* geared primarily toward developing winning products or services in the business world, but he recognizes that his suggestions apply equally well to relationships. He points out that the key to victory for companies is to "enchant" their customers, to delight them in a way that causes them to voluntarily change their hearts and their minds. Not manipulation, enchantment. Can you delight people? Sure. You can start with a smile, and you can follow it up a compliment, or a question about them, or their family. You can listen well. You can really listen to what people have to say. These are some of the simplest things you can do to be more giving and to enhance the quality of your relationships and the quality of your life.

Zingerman's Guide to Giving Great Service by Ari Weinzweig is a book on training to provide good service in a business setting. The fact is the whole concept of providing good customer service in business is to build strong, healthy relationships with customers. After all, no business can succeed without customers, and if your customers like you, it stands to reason that you will have more business from more customers. In this context, the book discusses the fact that life isn't fair. Weinzweig tells employees that in the world of service, **"Fair is another planet. And we, unfortunately, are not on it."** How true. Sometimes you may do something for someone that is not appreciated, and not even acknowledged. Don't let that keep you from continuing to be generous toward others. The blessings are real. We have the data that proves this.

Here's another activity to put you in the giving mindset. Imagine it is the afternoon of 9/11 and you are in the city of New York. People around you have been stunned by the morning's events with the collapse of the World Trade Center Towers. Nerves are raw and people have no way of knowing whether there may be more attacks to follow. Address those around you with a genuine concern for their feelings and their well-being. See how this mindset encourages you to be more than superficial when you greet others and ask how they are doing. Take this on in the next twenty-four hours and write out your thoughts about this activity.

In his book *The Pleasure Principle*, Paul Pearsall invites readers to develop awareness and control of selfish tendencies by using what he refers to as a "Polynesian pronoun" exercise. Spend an entire day without using the pronouns, "I, me, or mine." In situations where you would normally use such words, substitute other words or don't say anything at all. You will naturally spend time asking others about how they feel, what they want, and how you might help them. Pay attention to the use of these "self" words by others, and see if they begin to mirror your vocabulary by lessening their own use of these words. See if this doesn't make for a very enjoyable day as you focus on those around you rather than your own self-centered thoughts.

With all of this being said, the point is there's an infinite amount of value to be revealed in finding the elements of service that exist in the things that we already do. For those of us who may complain about going to work because we wish we had a different job, it's helpful to acknowledge that with whatever job we do, we are able to put food on the table and pay the rent or mortgage for ourselves and our family. In this sense, each minute we spend on the job is spent in service. And there's value in service at every level. Service is kindness.

Can we ever be too kind? Think of the transformation we will see when everyone becomes kinder. The implications are enormous. This calls to mind the words of Jimi Hendrix: "When the power of love overcomes the love of power the world will know peace." You can start by simply being more present to the service you already provide to others and helping others to do the same.

Most parents will call parenting the most challenging and fulfilling task on earth. What is parenting? At its core, it's a lifetime commitment to unselfish giving. You bring this new life into the world, and you are responsible for what becomes of your child. Young children rely on their parents for virtually everything. This makes everyday life an ongoing service experience.

In a *Time* magazine article, Joe Klein chronicles the story of a service organization called The Mission Continues, which engages veterans in service projects around the country:

There was absolutely no way Ian Smith was suffering from post traumatic stress disorder. He was sure of it.

He was O.K. He was living with his girlfriend in a suburb of Nashville working three jobs — mowing lawns, delivering pizzas, cleaning a local church. He was carrying a 4.0 average at Volunteer State Community College. Yes, he'd seen some terrible stuff during two tours in Iraq. But others had been through much worse. He'd never been wounded. He was alive.

But it was a strange sort of alive. He lived on his couch, with his pistol. He didn't sleep much. The only way he could get to sleep was by getting drunk, so he got drunk every night and slept with his gun under the pillow. He had gained 60 lb. since leaving the Army in February 2009. He drank more and more. His girlfriend left him. He put the gun to his head several times. "He absolutely refused to believe he was suffering from PTSD," said his buddy Mike Pereira, a fellow Army intelligence analyst. "But I wasn't going to let him alone."

Pereira was working for a veterans' service organization called the Mission Continues, in St. Louis. He heard Ian's anguish over the phone and over the headset when they played Call of Duty together. Mike had lived through some tough times too after leaving the Army. He too had been living alone, on the couch. He too had put a gun to his head. But he was living with a purpose now. And he kept after Ian to come to St. Louis: Come for a weekend, come do a service project. Mike talked nonstop about the Mission Continues and its leader, Eric Greitens, about the peace he'd found. Ian was skeptical —it almost sounded like a cult —but he agreed to visit Mike and work on a service project, cleaning up the Edgewood Children's Center in St. Louis.

And there, almost without noticing it at first, Ian began to feel better. He was painting a room with a bunch of veterans, trading war stories. "All of them had this real tough, kind of like, exterior, but inside they were just like me, just confused and scared and really angry," Ian, now 30, recalled. "And I saw these guys doing these very simple things. Nobody can argue with helping to paint a wall for a disabled or homeless kid. That's just good. There's no bad in that."

Ian went back to Mike's place and really slept that night, for the first time in months. "I was blown away by how much better I felt," Ian recalled. "And I thought, man, if I could just capture a little bit of that and hold it close to my heart, I think I could do all right. Things could get better."

Things got better. Ian moved to St. Louis. He lost the 60 lb. He stopped drinking so much; he moved the gun from his bed to the night table. He applied for and received a six-month public-service fellowship from the Mission Continues, and then joined the staff as a service-project coordinator. He was so successful at this that he was eventually summoned to the White House, to serve as an intern with Joining Forces, Michelle Obama's effort to help Iraq- and Afghanistan-war veterans. He is now completing a degree in international studies at Washington University in St. Louis.

This is a compelling turnaround story based on a commitment to service. In a study of the participants of this program, fully 86 percent reported a positive life-changing experience. If service can bring veterans back from the disturbed daze of PTSD, think of what it can do for those of us looking to overcome our day-to-day troubles.

Monday is a great day to make service day. We can connect with service one minute at a time. Be in giving mode. Concentrate on doing something to make someone feel good for at least sixty seconds. This can be done by complimenting or acknowledging someone in a special way. This can best be done face-to-face, but can also be by phone, text, email, or any other form of communication. You can also physically help someone with a task of some sort, even if it's something they would normally do themselves without help. For this to be true service, you should expect nothing in return. You want to simply experience the joy of unbridled giving. This is a great way to start off your week.

Some of the giving I learn about in my courtroom is marvelous. A family with four children took in a toddler who had been badly burned. The child's wounds required regular dressing changes every few hours for months. The foster mother, with the support of her family, cared for this child and the family eventually adopted her. She and her husband have given their children a timeless lesson in giving. In another case, two parents adopted three profoundly mentally impaired girls who require assistance with all of their basic living skills. Amazing.

Coming to understand the truth about giving and to fully embrace it is an ongoing journey. The benefits are massive. Serving gets us out of our own head and our own problems and connects us with the world of those around us in the most positive way. We have only the best of life to gain. When we really connect with giving, it's like throwing a stone in the water and catching a wave off the ripples. Serving is giving. Giving is living. What more can we ask for?

○⊂⊃ POINTS TO REMEMBER: ⊂⊃○

- The only thing that matters when we're gone, the only thing that counts, is what we've done for others.
- The quality of our lives is a function of the quality of our relationships. And there is no better way to build our relationships than to give.
- Charitable work literally makes the heart grow stronger.

- They who give have all things; they who withhold have nothing.
- You already have an unlimited supply of the greatest gifts to give to others.
- Fair is another planet, and we are not on it.

THE JOY IDENTITY

Happiness is not the absence of problems; it's the ability to deal with them.
—Steve Maraboli

Those who are happiest are those who do the most for others.
—Booker T. Washington

Love is sacrifice. When you love, sacrifice is easy.
And when you really love, sacrifice is joy.
—Gramma Roxie Owens

When man serves God, he has reached that point where he
doth serve himself best, and enjoys himself most.
—Charles H. Spurgeon

There is nothing either good or bad, but thinking makes it so.
—William Shakespeare

What do most Nobel Laureates, innovative entrepreneurs, artists and performers, well-adjusted children, happy couples and families, and the most successfully adapted mammals have in common? They play enthusiastically throughout their lives.
—**Stuart Brown**, National Institute for Play

P ower emanates from joy. When we are joyous, we are freed of the beasts of burdens. We have more energy. We are more aligned with the natural energy flow of the universe. Finding ways to amplify the joy in our lives is a powerful way to be. And who doesn't want to be happy? Or happier? So if we want to "be" more powerful, we need to find and master ways to be happy. Just as joy brings power, so too power in the hands of a person of integrity and compassion brings joy.

Why does power bring joy? The fact is power allows us to be more giving. It gives us more to work with when we reach out to help others, and this in turn makes us even happier. So, with joy and power and giving working together, we have an opportunity to tap into an extremely positive cycle. We get happier, we get more confident, confidence leads to power, as we become more powerful we have more to give, and as we give we become even happier, and on, and on, and on.

Contrary to what you may have come to believe, happiness is not like winning the lottery. Some are lucky to have it and some are not. **The fact is happiness is not "out there." It's "in here." It's an inside job.** It's not something we acquire. It's something we come to know. There are things that we can learn that will help us come to know it, but we can't buy it and no one can give it to us. No person and no property or amount of money can make us happy. Yet, we can design ourselves for happiness. And why shouldn't we? Especially when we think of what comes with it.

Earlier we discussed the three lies of identity. **The big lie of happiness is that money, fame, or achievements will make us happy.** As Professor Sonja Lyubomirsky, one of the foremost researchers in the field of happiness, points out, studies show that 50 percent of individual differences in happiness are determined by genes, 10 percent by life circumstances, and 40 percent by our intentional activities. Life circumstances refer to where we live, what kind of job and income we have, and other conditions of life. In other words, that promotion, or new house, or spouse you've been longing for is only going to impact 10 percent of your happiness at best. This is why studies of lottery winners find no significant gain in overall happiness one year after winning. This doesn't mean you wouldn't be thrilled to win, but over time your happiness will return to what it was. This is such an illuminating point. **We don't need to "chase" happiness, we need to "be" happy. We need to adopt intentional activities that will push us to be 40 percent happier.** That's where the real action is on the happiness front.

We tend to get caught up in the "comparison" game, thinking "if I was rich like him, or beautiful like her, or talented like them I would be happy," but these thoughts miss the point. **The fact is the happiest people in the world are not the richest, or the smartest, or the prettiest, they're not the strongest, or the most talented or famous. The happiest people in the world are the most giving people.** They feel more joy because they give more. They're "giving" gives them meaningful happiness, not temporary pleasure. And they know how to find joy in small doses. We don't experience grand events on a daily basis. To be happy on a daily basis we need to see the real joy there is in small moments, especially in giving and gratitude.

Happiness is a skill. Happy people know this. They know the kinds of things to do to make themselves happy, and more than that, they know the kinds of things to think about to be happy. They know what to pay attention to and what not to pay attention to, and this is the real difference maker. As you think about the concepts we are covering in this chapter and throughout this book, remember that everything you practice, you get better at. So, when you think about being happier and you do any of the things that are reported to bring more happiness, like helping others, you are going to get better at being happy.

Happiness comes with a host of benefits, things we might not specifically realize. There's actually more to happiness than just being able to wear a smile and to feel good. Consider this passage from Professor Lyubomirsky's book, *The How of Happiness: A Scientific Approach to Getting the Life You Want*:

It turns out that happiness brings with it multiple fringe benefits. Compared with their less happy peers, happier people are more sociable and energetic, more charitable and cooperative, and better liked by others. Not surprisingly then, happier people are more likely to get married and to stay married and to have richer networks of friends and social support.

Furthermore, contrary to Woody Allen's suggestion in Annie Hall that happy people are "shallow and empty, and . . . have no ideas and nothing interesting to say," they actually show more flexibility and ingenuity in their thinking and are more productive in their jobs. They are better leaders and negotiators and earn more money. They are more resilient in the face of hardship, have stronger immune systems, and are physically healthier. Happy people even live longer.

In sum, across all the domains of life, happiness appears to have numerous positive by-products that few of us have taken the time to really understand. In becoming happier, we not only boost experiences of joy, contentment, love, pride, and awe but also improve other aspects of our lives: our energy levels, our immune systems, our engagement with work and with other people, and our physical and mental health. In becoming happier, we bolster as well our feelings of self-confidence and self-esteem; we come to believe that we are worthy human beings, deserving of respect. A final, and perhaps least appreciated plus, is that if we become happier, we benefit not only ourselves but also our partners, families, communities, and even society at large.

Dr. Barbara Fredrickson, the Kenan Distinguished Professor of Psychology at the University of North Carolina at Chapel Hill, and a leading researcher of positive emotions, reports on research that illustrates that the degree to which we experience positive emotions predicts whether people languish or flourish. In other words, if you want to do well, if you want to excel, you need to get yourself to the happy farm and camp out.

So, we have something that makes us more powerful, popular and productive, healthier and wealthier, confident and resilient, and makes the people around us feel better too, and it's called happiness. What's not to like? And remember, anytime you're happy, you effectively crowd out the whole host of various negative feelings that can paint you into a dark corner. You can't be angry, depressed, worried or frustrated when you're happy. The more happiness you dial up, the more you dial down all of these negative feelings.

Let's look at some of the specific evidence that happiness at work leads to greater productivity and success. In *Authentic Happiness*, psychologist Martin Seligman discusses research he conducted on 272 employees over an 18-month period. His study indicates happier people get better performance evaluations and higher pay. A large study in Australia also linked happiness to higher income.

In *The Pursuit of Happiness*, David G. Myers states that happy employees are more efficient and have lower medical costs and less absenteeism than those who are depressed or unhappy. Further support comes from articles by J.M. George in *Human Relations*, and P. Totterdell and colleagues in the *Journal of Personality and Social Psychology*. They indicate a positive mood stimulates creativity, tolerance, and constructive, generous attitudes. A positive mood puts the focus on what is right as opposed to a negative mood that puts the focus on what is wrong. And happier people are more giving of their money, time, and energy. This is also supported in the article "How Workplace Happiness Can Boost Productivity" by Ray Williams.

In research at the University of Warwick, Associate Professor Daniel Sgroi measured significant gains in math performance when individuals were shown a ten-minute comedy clip. There you have it, a measurable justification for watching comedy. You've got work to do? Start a laugh-in. Does it make you more intelligent? Not necessarily, but it induces a mood or state that allows you to be more effective, to perform more intelligently. It greases the wheels. Harvard professors Teresa Amabile and Steven Kramer report in *Bloomberg Businessweek* that individuals who are happier on a given day are not only more likely to come up with a new idea or solve a complex problem that day, but the next day too.

Play and laughter are naturally associated with happiness. Play involves a host of activities that are basic components of learning such as curiosity, discovery, risk taking, trial and error, and other increasingly complex adaptive activities. Vigorous play triggers endorphins that lift our spirits. This relieves stress, pain, and fear. Playing with others fosters our sense of connection and reduces loneliness. Play also fosters perseverance. Playing with others for fun brings joy, vitality, and resilience to our relationships. Play encourages us to try new things and can improve all our relationships and our social skills. Think of how play teaches children to be with others, to work together, follow rules, and socialize in groups. These benefits continue for adults, and evidence suggests that play can reduce violence. Play provides an opportunity to develop positive, fulfilling relationships to replace negative beliefs, heal emotional wounds, and address issues of self-esteem.

Children who feel they are "playing" at everything are more successful and happier than those who feel they are working. In a study of attitudes, researchers found that some preteen children called almost everything they did "play," and others called almost everything they did "work." In a follow-up with these same children at the end of adolescence, the children who felt they were "playing" at everything were more successful and happier in school and more stable and content socially than those who felt they were working. As adults, we spend a great deal of time at work, and it's important that we play during work. Without some sense of recreation, productivity suffers. Success is not simply dependent on our time at work, but on the quality of our work. Quality depends on our sense of well-being.

There's even a recent trend in the appearance of ping-pong tables at offices. Dr. Daniel Amen, a renowned member of the American Board of Psychiatry and Neurology, indicates that table tennis specifically:

- Increases concentration and alertness
- Stimulates brain function
- Develops tactical thinking skills
- Develops hand/eye coordination
- Provides aerobic exercise
- Provides social and recreational interaction

This is an impressive list of benefits for something as simple as a ping-pong table. Workers who play note the speed with which they can build relationships at work by playing with their colleagues. When you are involved in playing a game with someone, you are connecting on a different level. Both players access a side of themselves that might otherwise be absent at work. The game itself serves as a medium of sorts, a channel of communication.

Playing at work in general:

- Keeps you functional when under stress
- Refreshes your mind and body
- Encourages teamwork
- Helps you see problems in new ways
- Triggers creativity and innovation

Mihaly Csikszentmihalyi, a writer and psychiatrist, authored a book called *Flow: The Psychology of Optimal Experience*. He suggests that people are happiest, not when they're "chillin' " or partying, but when they are in a state of flow—a state of complete concentration or absorption in a particular activity. **Flow is a state in which you are so involved in what you're doing that nothing else matters.**

One of the key characteristics of this state is a suspension of the normal sense of time, as though what you are doing is so engaging that you lose track of time and could go on indefinitely. Classic examples include a musician playing jazz, an athlete playing a sport, a filmmaker or record producer editing a film or mixing a song, a doctor performing surgery, and a performer of any kind engaged in their performance. Some of these activities would be more traditionally categorized as "play" than others. But they share a challenge for the individual, and an opportunity to display and build upon a growing talent or ability, regardless of what level a person is at. Flow requires a balance between the challenge of the task and the skill of the individual. If a task is too hard or too easy, one becomes overwhelmed or bored.

Csikszentmihalyi describes flow as "being completely involved in an activity for its own sake. The ego falls away. Time flies. Every action, movement and thought follows inevitably from the previous one, like playing jazz. Your whole being is involved, and you're using your skills to the utmost." By definition, when one is in flow, one is in the moment. There's a sense of clarity, confidence, and serenity, and an intrinsic motivation to stay in the moment and keep the action going. The more time you spend in a flow state, the richer your life is. Consider what activities constitute a state of flow for you. Engage yourself in one of your favorite flow activities for a half-hour. DO THIS NOW.

Reflect on what it's like to be in a flow state. Many of us have activities that trigger a flow state, but we don't spend as much time engaged in these activities as we could because we simply are too distracted. Television and Internet surfing are examples of things that occupy our time when we could be in flow, doing something we find much more absorbing and rewarding. Think about how you can structure your day and budget your time to be in flow for some time each day. Playing music or sports, drawing, writing, cooking, and making crafts are just a few examples of activities that might induce a state of flow for you. Flowing is living.

Bernie DeKoven is one of the originators of the New Games Movement. He has devoted his life to developing games that are designed to bring people together emotionally by simply playing for fun. If you've forgotten how to play, Bernie has some basic advice:

> You don't have to have rules or goals or a board or even anything to play with except each other. But whatever it is that you're playing, there are two things you have to take seriously: being together, and the sheer fun of it all. No game is more important than the experience of being together, being joined, being equal—governed by the same rules—playing for the same purpose. And no purpose is more uniting and freeing than the purpose of being fun with each other.

There's some insightful advice here. You have to take seriously the experience of being together and the sheer "fun of it all." That may be great advice for gaming, but it actually applies whenever you're doing just about anything with anyone. As we noted above, the more we can make a game of something, the more we can inject a sense of play and togetherness into anything we do, the better we'll do it and the more we'll enjoy it.

One of the most obvious ways to feel joy is to feel gratitude. We can always find something to be grateful for. When we are feeling grateful, we just don't have room to be angry, frustrated, or depressed in that moment. When we are truly grateful, that is; there's no room for darkness in a moment of gratitude. Even when a loved one dies, we can be grateful that they lived and that we knew them in life. Gratitude is a choice just as choosing to be happy is. You can choose not to be grateful, but if you do then don't expect to be happy.

If we're going to be happy, we have to be accepting. We have to accept where we are at, and any of our imperfections. As my former yoga instructor, Mary Ella, was fond of saying, **"We are all perfectly imperfect."** If you don't accept where you're at, at some level, you are starting out with a built-in sense of frustration and dissatisfaction that is going to sap your power. Even if you are looking to make major changes, start by accepting yourself as someone who has the power to make the changes you desire and is starting to do so. This allows you to work from a foundation of acceptance rather than a foundation of frustration. It's been said that self-love is critical to happiness and self-love has to start with acceptance.

What else can we do to boost our happiness? We can be fit. We can exercise. We can eat life-giving food. This is fairly obvious given all the research on the benefits of exercise and eating well, but, like many of the concepts we have discussed, too many people are missing out on the obvious benefit here. Millions of words and thousands of books have taken on the subjects of healthy eating and exercise, and as important as this is, an extended discussion is beyond the scope of this work. However, a few simple observations are in order. First of all, many will tell you that fitness is complicated, but before you accept that, remember that statement itself is a belief that you can accept or reject based on whether you consider it to be empowering or not.

What we refer to as exercise is essentially "movement" of one type or another. When we look at our bodies, it's easy to see that they were designed to move in thousands of ways. So, move! Find many ways of moving that are enjoyable to you and get to it. It can be sports, or walking, or biking, or swimming, or dancing, or anything, but we all need to be moving, and the more we like something, the easier it is to get ourselves to do it. The more you move, the more you're going to enjoy your life. It's as basic as that.

As for eating well, what we refer to as food is admittedly a bit more complicated these days. The bad news is we've gone from the natural food sources that we relied on just a hundred years ago, of things that grow, run, swim, and fly, to things that are created in factories with substances like chemicals, plastic, petroleum products, and synthetics as "ingredients." It's debatable whether we can actually call these things food at all, yet they fill the shelves of our supermarkets. And we have "Food Marts" where the only natural food that can be found is a highly salted bag of nuts.

What passes for food these days is anything that a multinational corporation can concoct that has a taste that people crave. This means massive amounts of sugar, salt, and fat have worked their way into today's food. And now that the backlash has begun as we have reached an obesity rate of almost 35 percent in the United States, according to the Centers for Disease Control and Prevention, you might think our food companies would treat us with more care. While there are certainly some real improvements, such as the use of whole grains rather than enriched flour in many products, we are also suffering new damage as food companies attempt to allow us to "have it all." We now have more artificial sweeteners and fats designed to give us the taste without the calories. And studies are now revealing these foods are even worse for our health than the real thing, the real sugars and fats that is. Imagine that.

While I'm not a nutritionist, I can share this basic recommendation. Be real, and eat things that are real, and use some common sense. And if you can discipline yourself to chew each bite of food forty times, as recommended, you will kill the tendency to overeat with this one simple strategy.

We have already discussed the joy that comes with service, the joy that comes to those who give. Giving is one thing that is always an option, even if it's a simple comment or compliment. You can never have too much giving or too much love in your life. Happiness also comes to us when we stop "resisting" and we allow ourselves to go with the flow. It's very easy to get caught up thinking about all the things that we don't want or the things we're unhappy with, but where does that get us? We need to pay attention to the moment we're in and what we're doing. We need to stop living as if it's only the next moment or tomorrow that really counts. We can check in with ourselves regularly and ask ourselves if we are resisting or if we are free.

Think about when you're on vacation. You've been released from your normal work duties, and everything is a lighthearted adventure. What if you just carried that attitude with you to work? Take a day at work this week and walk in as if you're walking onto a cruise ship. If you can wear something to symbolize your vacation mindset, all the better. See if you can encourage others to mirror your attitude, with or without explaining the game. And if you find it too difficult to imagine yourself on vacation while you're at work, imagine you're at work the day before you leave for a two-week trip to Hawaii or whatever favorite vacation spot you would like to conjure. If this sounds like a game, it is. Enjoy it.

What about laughter? Take all the benefits we've talked about for happiness and multiply them times eight. A good laugh is a tonic for pretty much anything, and a great laugh is a marvelous experience that you can relish forever. Laughter literally shakes us up in a fundamentally positive way. We've all experienced this. Humor and laughter not only strengthen our immune systems, they boost our energy, reduce pain, and relieve us from the damaging effects of stress.

Helpguide.org, a nonprofit resource, outlines the benefits in an article, "Laughter Is the Best Medicine." Laughter relaxes the body and relaxes muscles for up to forty-five minutes. It decreases stress hormones and increases immune cells, improving your natural defense system. Laughter releases endorphins, our natural feel-good chemicals, and increases blood flow, reducing the risk of heart attacks and cardiovascular problems. And those are just the physical benefits. As for mental benefits, laughter brings a sense of joy to life, reduces anxiety, improves mood, and enhances our resilience. Laughter is so powerful that cancer treatment centers have formed laughter clubs in which patients laugh together to induce all of these physical and mental benefits.

Cancer and laughter? Seriously? Can cancer be cured by a series of laughing spells? While it might sound strange, it certainly could be an empowering belief to have. And if you're going to die, as we all are, isn't it better to die laughing?

Lee Berk, an assistant professor of family medicine and researcher in complementary and alternative medicine at the University of California, Irvine, led a study that found that levels of stress hormones were reduced, and levels of endorphins were increased, not only from laughter itself, but from simply anticipating a funny event.

As reported at HealingCancerNaturally.com/laughter-is-medicine.html, researchers tracked hormone levels after individuals were simply told they were going to watch a funny movie, and the researchers were able to note measurable improvements in these hormone levels. While this may sound surprising, the fact is it's consistent with everything we've said throughout this program of identity design. When you focus on something good, even if it's a funny movie, you feel good. Your thoughts impact you more than anything else, and we are working on channeling those thoughts to be happier. So the next time you need a boost, you can think about a funny movie and plan to see it as soon as you can!

Having a really great laugh with someone is a unique bonding experience. When I think of a number of my friends, the thing I tend to remember the most is things that we've laughed about. I think about experiences where we connected in our own way about something with our own unique spin. Laughter is a communal activity. Think of how much more readily we laugh at something when we are with someone than when we are alone. In one survey, laughter was observed to be thirty times more frequent in social situations than when individuals were alone.

You might think that you can only laugh when something spontaneously hits you as really funny, but you can set yourself up to laugh more frequently. Watching comedies, reading comics, humor books, and articles, spending time with funny friends, and playing with children are just a few things you can do to laugh more. With Internet sites like YouTube, performances of virtually any comedian or comedy group or show are at our fingertips.

Funny is a mindset like everything else. And the more you "practice" seeing things as funny, the better you'll be at it. When you set your mind to it, you really can start laughing at all kinds of things in this absurd world of ours. **Spend a day thinking of yourself as a comedian who finds something funny about everyday things.**

In *59 Seconds,* Richard Wiseman cites an experiment in which people were asked to describe on paper the most wonderful experience in their lives. Three months later, in comparison with a control group, these individuals were significantly happier. In another study, people who regularly listed five things that they were grateful for ended up happier, more optimistic, and healthier.

Sam Berns, a seventeen-year-old who lives with the disease progeria, presented his three principles for living a happy life in a TedxMidAtlantic 2013 talk, which can be viewed on YouTube, http:YouTube.com/watch?v=36m1o-tM05g. Progeria is a disease that afflicts children with advanced aging resulting in growth failure, hair loss, stiff joints, aged-looking skin, osteoporosis, and atherosclerosis cardiovascular disease. Children with the disease die of heart attacks or strokes at an average of thirteen years of age.

In spite of this disease, which limits his ability to do many things a normal seventeen-year-old would be able to do, Sam states unequivocally that he lives a happy life. He cites three basic principles: First, to accept the things that you ultimately can't do because there is so much that you can do. Second, surround yourself with people you want to be around. Third, keep moving forward. One of his favorite quotes is from Walt Disney (*Meet the Robinsons*): "Around here . . . we don't look backwards for very long. We keep moving forward, opening new doors and doing new things . . . and curiosity keeps leading us down new paths." This is a fairly simple philosophy. Happiness is a skill. Following these principles is a sure way to develop this skill. Sam states that he consciously works to keep from feeling sorry for himself and still admits that he has bad days. When he has difficulty, he accepts it and looks for things to get better.

When I think about the challenge of really taking on this business of living, and living joyfully, I am reminded of a discussion about living on a cancer ward by Paul Pearsall in *The Pleasure Principle*. Pearsall lived on a cancer ward when he was receiving a bone marrow transplant. He notes that the residents were among the happiest people he had ever met. How could that possibly be? He relays the comments of a patient named Alice. She credits cancer patients with having what she calls "survivor's pleasure." She says, "Cancer patients are often less afraid of dying than of not being able to die when we must. Maybe that's why we find so much more in life. Dying isn't controlling our life anymore; enjoying being alive is. We know there are two parts to death: letting go of life and dying. When you think about the idea of letting go of life, it is like letting go of your child as he gets older and must leave. You don't want him to go, you know he must, so you're really trying to enjoy the time you have with him." With an insight such as this, it strikes me that we have it backward when we say people are dying of cancer. It seems more appropriate to say they are "living" of cancer.

I am also reminded of the conversation I had with Jim Cahaney, a dedicated Transcendental Meditation instructor I worked with when we established a pilot program to teach our high-risk offenders to meditate. He told me that when his mother was near the end of her life, she started giving away her things in a joyful way. It was as though she realized that the "things" of her life had nothing to offer her but the joy that may come from giving them away. How tragic it is to think that all of the joy of living is at our fingertips on a daily basis, yet it eludes us and slips through our fingers like so many grains of sand while we think about things we want that we don't have. We think about some other place we want to live, or some other person we want to be, or be with. Ask a cancer patient like Alice how essential any of these things are and she'll tell you . . . not much.

If you're not happy right now, ask yourself honestly why not. Why not this minute? Think about how much it has to do with what you're saying to yourself and look at that conversation.

In his book *The Joy of Selling*, Steve Chandler points out that we are always selling. A parent sells the concept of good behavior to their child, a teacher sells a subject to his student, a boss sells the concept of productivity to her employee, a waiter sells his service to a diner, a friend sells her companionship to a friend, and on, and on, and on. Selling makes the world go 'round. And how can you sell anything any better than when you're happy?

Chandler recommends salespeople listen to some favorite music, or start their day with a call to someone who they always enjoy talking to, so they can be in the right mood to approach their clients. Think about how much better you respond to people when they're in an upbeat, happy mood. You want to be around people like that, and others will want to be around you when you're in a happy mood. So, it stands to reason that any client will feel more comfortable with someone who is happy. It's fairly obvious, but we don't generally think of this because we're so busy with the work we have to do or the things we have to worry about. If you want to sell something, **sell yourself on the idea of being happy all the time.** And even if you're not happy "all the time," being happy "more" of the time will pay real dividends.

When we're happy, we can do just about anything better and enjoy ourselves while we're doing it. We could formulate this as follows:

$$A + J = OR$$
Action + Joy = Optimum Result

The reverse would be:

$$A - J = LTOR$$
Action – Joy = Less Than Optimum Result

Add into this equation the effect that joy has on our health. Here's another metaphor we can use to connect with this concept: Our immune system is our body's defense system. Any virus that could make us sick has to do so by breaking through or getting past our immune system. The stronger our immune system is, the more difficult it is to get sick because even if we're exposed to certain germs or viruses, our immune system can keep them from causing any damage and causing us to get sick.

Think of our immune system as a reservoir, a giant pool of water. Think of germs or viruses as little fires. The healthier our immune system is, the more water we have in our reservoir to put out any fires. You can visualize, or imaginize, a big bucket of water that can put out any flame. But if you don't have enough water in your reservoir to fill that bucket, you're at risk. Without enough water, you won't be able to put out that fire. A fire that you can't put out will spread. That's what happens with a virus that goes unchecked. It spreads and we get sick.

Now think about that reservoir. When you are happy, you are essentially feeding that reservoir that is your immune system. It's like you have a river that's feeding into it. The happier you are, the wider, deeper, and faster that river is that feeds into it. Think about people who you know who are happy all the time. You're likely to find that they just don't get sick very much because their immune system is so strong. That reservoir is always full and that feeder river is running strong. There's always plenty of water to put out any fires.

Now think about the opposite. Think about when you're not happy. Think about when you're under stress, when you're worried, when you're miserable or depressed. Now, you not only have shut off that joyful feeder river, you've actually reversed its flow. Now, your stress and misery is actually draining your immune system reservoir. The longer you are miserable, or depressed, or angry, or feeling any negative emotion of any kind, the more you are draining that all important reservoir of your immune system. Your joy and your wellness are a cycle, and you need to keep it moving in the right direction, or you'll pay the consequences.

It's simply a lot harder to go through a day in a bad mood than in a good one. But most of us don't think about choosing our moods. We just think they are what they are. Nothing could be further from the truth. **Happy people are not lucky to be happy; they cultivate the joy in their lives.** They water the flowers and let the sunshine in. They can recognize small favors, simple things to be grateful for. They don't spend time obsessing over things they don't have, but celebrate what they do have. Sam Berns, who we discussed earlier, insists on focusing on what he can do rather than on the things that he can't. He lets the sunshine in.

What can you do to let the sunshine in? What are some things you can focus on or think about that make you happy? If I ask you what can you do right now to make yourself happy, what will your answer be? If your answer is "Buy a new pair of shoes," please go back to the beginning of this book and start over.

Think about someone who just never seems to be happy about anything, someone who is always complaining and is generally miserable. Why do you think they act the way that they do? They've adopted a view of the world where everything is wrong, or at least everything that they think about is wrong. If you want to look for things to complain about, there's certainly no shortage there, but this turns life into a miserable experience. This leaves us in a nonresourceful state. When we are frustrated, miserable, angry, or depressed, we need to shift to a resourceful state. One thing you can get in the practice of doing is to ask yourself, "What's the most loving thing I can do for myself right now?" For example, get a glass of water or take a break to walk outside for a moment. Ask yourself this once a day and follow through (within reason), and see if you don't find yourself feeling significantly better.

Researchers with the Institute of HeartMath and other entities have shown that the human heart communicates with the body in unique ways. **This research shows that the heart has its own brain, the heart brain, which sends messages to the rest of the body in four specific ways.** These messages are transmitted to the brain in our head as well as the rest of the body. An article titled "Heart-Brain Interactions," published by the Institute of HeartMath, lays out the biological format for the heart's powerful and diverse messaging system. IHM researchers explain these findings in "Science of the Heart," an overview of research conducted by the institute: "Research has shown that the heart communicates to the brain in four major ways: neurologically (through the transmission of nerve impulses), biochemically (via hormones and neurotransmitters), biophysically (through pressure waves) and energetically (through electromagnetic field interactions)."

One important way the heart can speak to and influence the brain is when the heart is coherent—experiencing stable, sine-wavelike pattern in its rhythms. When the heart is coherent, the body, including the brain, begins to experience all sorts of benefits, among them greater mental clarity and ability, including better decision making. These changes come about because the heart, when it is coherent, sends out information that causes the changes via the processes mentioned above—neurologically, biochemically, biophysically and energetically.

Although the heart and brain are automatically in constant communication, each of us also has in our capacity to consciously and intentionally direct our hearts to communicate in beneficial ways with our bodies. When we intentionally experience sincere positive emotions such as caring, compassion, or appreciation for someone or something, the heart processes these emotions and begins to become coherent and send out positive information throughout the entire body.

When people say that you need to "follow your heart" to be happy, there's scientific support for this very statement. And we see here the specific reference to caring and compassion, which are key components of the service identity. What this means is that everything we've said about self-talk and the conversation that we have with ourselves that shapes our identity is not just a conversation going on in our head. Our heart is a vital part of the conversation as we can see from the information here. The heart brain, or the heart mind, isn't an esoteric scientific theory; it's something we can feel. We've all felt real pain and real joy. Where? In our heart.

We've talked about happiness as a skill. When we look at all the benefits that come with it, we can see that in many ways it really is the ultimate life skill. It's not only the best feeling we can have, it makes us better at everything we do.

Happiness makes us feel:

- Great
- Healthier
- Wealthier
- More powerful
- More productive
- More popular
- More confident
- More content
- More cooperative
- More constructive
- More creative
- More flexible
- More generous
- More grateful
- More energetic
- More engaging
- More resilient
- And more loving

If you want to be better at just about anything, start with being "more happy." To be "more happy," use the strategies laid out here or develop your own. Success will follow.

- Focus on gratitude and generosity.
- Listen to your heart.
- Focus on funny.
- Recognize life for the game that it is and play.

- Focus on what you can do, not on what you can't do.
- Spend time with people you love, and people who love you, and tell them you love them.
- Keep moving forward.
- Find activities that put you in a state of flow.
- Do more of all of these things and less of all the things that distract you from these things, and watch your world as it warms up and begins to shine.
- Develop your joy from the inside and let it shine on the outside. Rely on your own joy generator. Most of all, work to make others happy and let that bring you joy rather than counting on others to make you happy.

These are proven strategies which you can use to be happier now. Concentrate on one a day to find which are most helpful to you and to assimilate the most helpful practices into your daily life. As you do you'll find you're happier already!

○▭ POINTS TO REMEMBER: ▭○

- Happiness is not "out there." It's "in here." It's an inside job. Happiness is a skill.
- The big lie of happiness is that money, fame, or achievements will make us happy.
- We don't need to "chase" happiness, we need to "be" happy. We need to adopt intentional activities that will push us to be 40 percent happier.
- The fact is the happiest people in the world are not the richest, or the smartest, or the prettiest, they're not the strongest, or the most talented or famous. The happiest people in the world are the most giving people.
- Happiness is a skill.
- Children who feel they are "playing" at everything are more successful and happier than those who feel they are working.
- Flow is a state in which you are so involved in what you're doing that nothing else matters.
- We are all perfectly imperfect.
- You can think of yourself as a comedian who finds something funny about everyday things.

- Sell yourself on the idea of being happy all the time.
- A + J = OR   Action + Joy = Optimum Result
- A – J = LTOR   Action – Joy = Less Than Optimum Result
- Happy people are not lucky to be happy; they cultivate joy in their lives.
- The heart has its own brain, the heart brain, which sends messages to the rest of the body in four ways.
- When people say you need to "follow your heart" to be happy, there's scientific support for this statement.
- If you want to be better at just about anything, start with being "more happy." To be "more happy," use the strategies laid out here or develop your own. Success will follow.

THE PLANNING IDENTITY

A good plan today is better than a perfect plan tomorrow.
—Extrapolated from a quote by **General George S. Patton**

Always plan ahead. It wasn't raining when Noah built the ark.
—Richard C. Cushing

If you plan to win as I do, the game never ends.
—Stan Mikita

It takes time to save time.
—Joe Taylor

It's not the plan that is important, it's the planning.
—Graeme Edwards

There is in the act of preparing, the moment you start caring.
—Winston Churchill

First you write down your goal; your second job is to break down your goal into a series of steps, beginning with steps which are absurdly easy.
—Fitzhugh Dodson

Do you have a plan? We can't expect to get anywhere if we don't have a plan. People without a plan get used by people who have one. Your life is meant be just that—YOURS. To have an effective plan you need to decide where you want to go, how you're going to get there, and then take action to make it happen. Your life is in your hands when you have a plan.

Where are you going? If you don't have a destination, any road will take you there. **People with plans make things happen.** People without plans are left to react to what happens around them. It's the difference between being a pinball being bounced from pillar to post, and being the pinball wizard who is flipping the levers and controlling when, where, how fast, and how hard. **Would you rather be the pinball or the pinball wizard?** Are you here to make something happen or are you just hoping you can get through the day without getting run over?

A failure to plan is a plan for failure. In order to get somewhere, you have to start with a destination. We will refer to this as a goal. There are, of course, short-term, mid-term, and long-term goals. There are things that can be accomplished in days, minutes, or years, depending on the goal. The key to accomplishment is to set a course and stay true to it. A journey of a thousand miles begins with a single step, but not just any step, a step in the right direction.

Most of the time when we drive somewhere, we know exactly where we're going. But if it's somewhere we've never been before, we wouldn't dream of not checking on our destination and mapping it out, or planning how to get there. (Although with the development of GPS, this analogy may sound dated. Map-reading skills have been rendered irrelevant to many. And while I realize the map is not the territory, reading the map helps prepare you for the territory.)

The life of your dreams is not going to show up unannounced at your doorway one day, so there's no point in waiting on the couch for the doorbell to ring. It's also not going to tap you on the shoulder as you hustle from one "urgent" task to another, making busy, without making a life. Massive action without direction is no better than inaction when it comes to forging the life of your dreams.

You have to dream it up, and then draw it up, and then start it up—meaning you first have to decide what it is, what it looks like. Then, you have to come up with a plan to make it happen. Your plan has to break everything down into manageable steps. Then, you have to take the first one and keep going, one by one, adjusting as needed along the way. That's the basic framework. And since life is meant to be moving and growing, once you reach your dreams, you're going to want to start over in one way or another.

Planning is intentional work. You are directing your intention when you plan. Planning is the ultimate proactive step. Why? Because when you're planning, you are taking time out to decide where you're going and how you're going to get there. Planning is the most important part of the job because it determines what the job is and how the job gets done.

An effective plan is a plan that works for you. There are general principles to guide us. **If you think you're too busy to plan, the fact is you're too busy not to.** You can think of it as simply setting an expectation about what you want to happen and how you'll make it happen. One way to start deciding where you want to go is to picture what a day in your life looks like when you get there.

It's time to pull your future into the present. This is not an exercise; this is a dream. A few things to remember: This is not someone else's future, it's yours. You don't need someone else's approval to reach for your dream. And this can be as much fun and as big as you're willing to make it. This is imaginization—creating a future in your mind and stepping into it in your life. At the moment, your first job is to plant the seeds for success; you don't need to worry about how you will accomplish everything. Just state a goal, a future which is compelling and exciting for you.

How to create a dream future? Imaginize. Let's start with five years. Five years from now, what are you doing? What do you have? Where do you live? What have you become? To answer these questions with clarity is the secret to creating your future. So, you wake up—where are you, who are you with, what do you have for breakfast, how do you spend your morning, who do you meet for lunch, and how do you spend your afternoon and evening? These answers will give you a definite picture, something to shoot for. And remember **if you're not shooting for something . . . you're shooting for nothing!**

The more specifically you draw the picture, the more energy it will bring you. And it's more than a picture. It's what you see, hear, feel, taste, touch, and smell in your fabulous future that draws you forward. We're talking about a future that springs you out of bed in the morning with the knowledge that each day that you stay on course, you're one day closer to all of it being real. And we need to recognize that this is the way that successful, prosperous, and happy people live. This is how they approach life. And they enjoy the journey more than the reaching of the destination.

Your planning can integrate the various concepts we've covered in this program, starting with the conscious development of your identity and the specific characteristics of identity work we've touched on. What would you like to do to pursue the shaping of your identity to live the life of your dreams? Take a moment to write out what plan you could start to implement immediately for this. You can draw on any of the ideas we've discussed throughout this program. DO THIS NOW.

To be effective in reaching any long-range goal, you need to break it down into steps. This can be done by backing up and imaginizing yourself one year from now, and ninety days from now. Once this is done and linked to specific dated performance objectives, which we'll discuss in a moment, you'll have benchmarks to measure your progress. In this context, progress is you making it happen. This is the essential part of planning.

One of the most important tools of successful people is their ability to set goals and pursue them, and we might say "persevere" them. But there is an important distinction to be made between "wishes" and "goals." Anyone, and in fact nearly everyone, would probably be willing to say, "I'd like to lose weight." But how many people have written down the specificity to say that "By January 1, 2016, I will weigh 180 pounds." People can say, "I'd like to have a new house." But it's different to say, "I will own a 2,000-square-foot home with three bedrooms and two baths by June 21, 2016." The key is that effective goals are specific and measurable. Let's take another example. Let's say you decided that you wanted set a goal to treat your spouse or your children or your parents better. What would be an example of a specific and measurable goal to address that? An example could be "I will thank my wife and/or compliment her twice a day for the next seven days."

When setting your goals, state your outcome in positive terms, be specific, and state a measurable result. In his book *Unlimited Power*, Anthony Robbins has suggested these great guidelines for effective goal setting. (The parenthetical comments are added.)

State your outcome in positive terms. Say what you want, not what you don't want. (This is an important point to maintain your attention in a progressive way. If you say you don't want to be fat, you're thinking about being fat. You're better off thinking about being fit and feeling great!)

Be as specific as possible. How does your outcome look, sound and feel? Set a specific completion date. (This is designed to inspire you to get moving and take action. If thinking about it doesn't get you motivated, then there's something wrong with your target. It could be that you see it as so far off that you don't really see yourself realistically obtaining it. If this is the case, you need to reset your belief system so you see it as realistic, or you need to set another target. It could also be that your target is something safe and secure, or something many other people might want, but something that doesn't really excite you. If this is the case, you have to open up the throttle and find something that's more inviting, something that makes you move.)

State a measurable result so you can tell when you've achieved your goal. (If you can't measure it, you tend to end up with commendable but amorphous statements like "I'm going to be a better parent." Great, but how do you measure your progress? These kinds of goals make it easy to saunter along without accomplishing anything because there's no marker to check your accountability. Instead, you could say, "I'm going to do something special to acknowledge my child every day.")

State an outcome that is initiated and maintained by you. State your outcome in a way that reflects things that you can affect directly. (Goals that are premised on manipulating people, or are dependent on someone else, are problematic. Being manipulative runs counter to all the principles of Identity Design. Your goal should be something that you can make happen. Let's say you work as a salesperson and want to sell twenty cars per month. You have to rely on purchasers deciding to make a purchase to actually close a sale, and while it's good to have a sales target, in that sense, this target, or goal, is not completely controlled by you. However, something that is completely in your control would be the number of sales calls that you make each day. Based on your daily call volume, you should experience a corresponding number of sales.)

Look at the consequences of reaching your goal and be sure the outcome is one that benefits you and others. (No man is an island, so if something is worthwhile then it should benefit both you and others. For example, educating yourself makes you more knowledgeable and marketable, and better able to make the world a better place.)

Once you've set your goals, you can't simply file them away somewhere and expect them to happen. You need to break them down into action steps. If you want a new car, you have to decide how you will pay for it. Will you finance it? How much will you borrow? Over what amount of time? What will you pay as interest? How long will you expect to have the car? Will it fit your budget for that period of time? How will you select which car to buy and how will you insure it? You may not initially have all the answers to these questions, so initially you may be just planning how to get the information to be able to answer these questions so you can then decide what car to get and how to pay for it.

For bigger goals, you need to post them somewhere such as on your desk or a bathroom mirror and review them daily, the more often the better. When you're working on a goal, **direction is more important than placement. We are always on the journey.**

You don't need to focus on how far you are from completion. You need to focus on the direction you're going. Are you moving toward it, standing still, or moving farther from completion? When you achieve one goal you'll start on another, so we need to remind ourselves that we are always on the journey. Every "destination" is merely a place along the road we travel throughout our lifetime. So while it's good to reach goals, remember that's the start of a new chapter.

If you haven't been in the practice of setting goals for yourself, you can start by setting some short-term achievable goals. You can think of goal achievement as a muscle: the more you work it, the stronger it gets. This builds confidence in your ability to make things happen. You should also think in terms of bigger long-term goals. Think of something that really excites you because this is where the real value of goal setting is. It's the ability to stretch yourself beyond your comfort zone to where your real growth potential lies. We grow when we are learning and when we are taking on things that are new to us. If we live each day in our comfort zone, doing the same things over and over, thinking the same thoughts over and over, we are not growing.

As we have noted throughout this program, the words we use are critical to the results we get. Another adjustment we can make here is to the ever-present "to do" list, that list that we have of the things that we believe we should do. If these are things we should do, then there are reasons we should do them. We go to work so we can pay the rent. We pay the rent so we have a place to sleep, etc. Why call it a "to do" list? Calling it that can associate everything on that list with a sense of drudgery. We don't like to live in drudgery, so we shouldn't talk to ourselves in a way that leads us to feel this way.

Why not simply rename this list of things we plan to do in a way so that we are encouraged to actually do them? **We don't need a "to do" list. We need a "to win" list.** Then, every time we think of our list, we are reminded not just that we have something to do, but that we will do it because when we do, we win. Everybody likes winning, and small victories lead to bigger ones. Make your "to do" list a "to win" list and start counting your victories. Let this simple shift remind you that as you've come to get to know who you are, you have come to identify things to do that are important to you. You are doing things that matter. Even small things are part of your productivity and part of your life.

Now that you've presented an initial plan, let's look at the various topics we've covered. You can review the identity questions that were presented earlier. Have you continued to ask yourself these questions? Have you continued to ask yourself who you are and who you want to be?

As we grow, the answers may change, but these questions are always important. Think of the three lies of identity we discussed. Have you been able to separate yourself from evaluating and identifying yourself based on what you have, what others think of you, and what you've done? Or are you still driving through life looking in the rearview mirror?

Do you feel like you're in the choosing business? Are you still asking yourself questions that are negative affirmations, questions that ask, "Why can't I . . .?"

How are you doing with your physical, mental, recreational, financial, and spiritual parts of your life?

Do you feel you're engaged in the process, in the journey of life?

Do you have a personal definition that empowers you and gives meaning to your life? What do you think about why you are here?

Do you feel you're in sync with your natural purpose, or do you feel resistance in your life that you have to work against?

Do you feel free and in control? Are you thinking about the consequences of the actions you are taking? Are you thinking about the people who you are spending time with and how they are influencing you?

What is your plan for increasing your sense of ownership in your life? Do you regularly look at the results in your life and claim responsibility for them?

This is a way of building your sense of power and control. Always recognize the fact that you are a cause in the matter of what shows up in your life. If something good shows up, you can take credit. If something bad shows up, such as a problem in one of your key relationships, then acknowledge that because you were a cause in whatever problem developed, you have the power to fix the problem.

Remind yourself that you are in the "choosing" business, and that you are choosing what you do, what you think, and what you feel. Stop complaining and arguing and making excuses about things, because this drains your power and your ownership. Accept that your life is uniquely designed for your benefit, and that the challenges you face are perfect challenges for you to have.

Claim ownership, responsibility, and control in your life. Accept where you are. Claim ownership over the relationships you have, and watch to see who influences you in a good way and who influences you negatively.

Recognize that any statement can be interpreted by any person in any way they choose, and claim ownership of your interpretations and ensure that they are empowering. Look at the world in a way that reflects your world as building and moving forward rather than falling apart and stagnating. Claim ownership of your communications with others and your communication with yourself.

What is your plan to increase your effectiveness in dealing with challenges? We have discussed at length the need to have the right attitude in the face of challenges. We need to develop our growth mindset. The growth mindset encourages us to take on more and more challenges because we know they push us to learn and develop. We don't see them as roadblocks or tests of our talent or ability that can impair our self-image. The growth mindset recognizes that it's good to be out of our comfort zone. We also need a plan to address the issue of our ongoing improvement. If we are going to continue to grow and develop, we need a strategy for that too. This will make us even more adaptable and will kill our worries as we become more and more welcoming of new challenges.

Have you adjusted your attitude regarding failure so that you no longer fear it and are no longer willing to let it hold you back?

Are you willing to take risks in the pursuit of happiness, recognizing that you can't always count on things going as planned, but knowing that you need to take your chances if you're going to live?

Have you come to peace with the fact that failure and rejection are part of the process of success, and are you willing to accept your fair share?

Are you willing to stop worrying about looking like a fool to chase your dreams?

Fear is a learned response. Have you unlearned this response, or is there a plan needed for this too? Fears arise with challenges, so as you welcome challenges, you kill the fears and the worries that they otherwise bring.

One of the most important and most overlooked aspects of planning is the planning we need to do to manage the countless distractions we face, which can keep us from accomplishing anything we want to do. Not too long ago it seemed that the main time bandit we faced was the television. We could just turn it on, and even if there was nothing we really wanted to watch, we could just keep flipping channels or channel surfing for an hour, which could turn into two or three or more. Now we have the Internet and its instant access to just about everything; and social media with its instant access to just about everyone, so some people feel pressured to just keep "posting" so that everyone will know what a fabulous life they're living. Is this any way to live? Managing our plans and reaching our goals means we have to be able to manage all of the "noise" that comes from these distractions. What it means is we have to plan our time!

Time is a zero-sum game. Thus, we need a "not to do" list. We need a list of things we need to stop doing so that we can do the things that do matter. At any given moment, our attention can really only be on one thing. The reason many of us are not where we want to be with our lives is because we're not optimizing our time and our attention. We are paying too much of our attention on things that don't really matter. The time we spend thinking about things that don't matter, such as mindlessly surfing the Internet, is time we can't devote to the things that are really important to us. Of course, a limited amount of this downtime is fine, but the problem is when we get trapped in unproductive patterns and time warps.

Research says we waste more time worrying than any other activity. Worry is the antithesis of being in the moment. There's nothing productive about worry. We might even say the quality of our life is directly related to our ability to eliminate the time we spend worrying. The less worrying we do, the more living we can do.

One response to address this issue and other time traps is what is referred to as a "not to do" list. On a list like this, you identify unproductive time traps that you need to eliminate so that you can stay on track and spend your time on things that are meaningful to you. A "not to do" list might include an item such as "no television watching" or "no more than an hour a day of television." We all know people who like to gossip endlessly, and just spending time with people like this can be a real time killer.

What are some time traps that you tend to fall in to? If you're really serious about getting things done, establishing your "not to do" list and following through can be just as important as your to-do list because it gives you time to do the things you need to. Make out a "not to do" list. DO THIS NOW.

Check in with your "not to do" list regularly. Keep it current and check your compliance with this list. New time traps will appear from time to time and this is a consciousness exercise that keeps you aware of the things you need to be on guard against. This is another way in which you take control of your life. And as we've noted repeatedly, identity design is about control.

While you might think of your dream as a specific career or financial goal, or some specific personal achievement, it really should be broader than that. Look for balance in your mental, physical, social, spiritual, and financial lives.

Don't hurry your planning. If you rush this stage, everything else is jeopardized by poor planning. If you are committed to something but you don't know how to accomplish each step, plan and start with what you know, with the confidence that as you move forward answers will come to you. As they say, when you are committed to something, "a path appears." A car can drive hundreds of miles through the dark while its headlights can only illuminate a few hundred feet at a time.

Some additional points for planning:

- Schedule uninterrupted time every day to plan!
- Plan for tomorrow tonight, and let your subconscious go to work on your project while you sleep.
- Write out your plan so you know what it is, you don't lose any of it, and you commit to it.
- If you don't know where you're going, you never know when you'll get there.
- Set a goal, and even if you take the smallest possible step, you'll be on your way.
- Direction is more important than placement.
- When you want to accomplish something, tell someone that you are going to do it.
- A couple of minutes each day, before you get out of bed, is a great time to mentally review the day to come and to set your expectations for what you'll do and how well things will go.

With a plan in hand, you are ready to begin your advance on the goals that you've set. One step at a time is really all that's required. This entire program is geared to support your adoption of constructive beliefs so you realize that whatever you decide to pursue, you have the power to achieve. That power is yours to go after anything that matters. I have a daily plan to establish and reinforce the key identity concepts developed here so you can live the life you choose.

The 7/60 Mad Minute Identity Design Plan

The concept of "mad minutes" was introduced in the first chapter. Now that you are familiar with the various concepts discussed here, we are ready to lay out the full 7/60 Mad Minute Identity Design Plan. I'll restate the overall concept and set the specific schedule that you will follow.

What can you do in sixty seconds? Sixty seconds of pure focus is a dynamic force at your command that can redefine your identity. The discipline to activate this force twice a day is available to anyone who chooses. A seven-day schedule geared to the construction and reinforcement of key elements of personal power will yield the identity you need in order to get the life you want. All you need is the belief and the will. **The 7/60 Mad Minute Plan is identity design for busy people. Start now.**

Rules of the game. As we pointed out earlier, those who recognize and identify their activities as "play" are more effective and happier than those who see things as "work." This says there's value in viewing life as a game. How are you doing? We're not asking for your score. We're not asking how much do you have. It's a question of mode. A question of feeling, of being.

We have a seven-day, sixty-second schedule to redefine your new identity by building on the concepts we've outlined here. Some of these concepts may already be strengths of yours and some of them may not be. Regardless of where your strengths and weaknesses are, this plan will initiate and reinforce power and confidence to make you more effective, productive, and happy in all areas of your life.

You're going to go on the clock for sixty-second intervals, once in the morning and once in the afternoon. We call these mad minutes, minutes in which nothing else matters. The key is to engage for at least one minute in which nothing else matters and nothing can stop you. If your daily schedule permits you to use a given time of day, in the morning and in the afternoon, that's fine. If not, you'll need to find that minute for yourself. The focus will be as follows:

Monday. Service day. For one minute in the morning and one minute in the afternoon, be of service. Be in giving mode. Concentrate on making someone feel good. This can be done by complimenting or acknowledging someone in a special way. This can best be done face-to-face, but can also be by phone, text, email, or any other form of communication. You can also physically help someone with a task of some sort, even if it's something they would normally do themselves without help. For this to be true service, you should expect nothing in return. You want to simply experience the joy of unbridled giving. This is a great way to start off your week.

Tuesday. Gratitude day. For one minute in the morning and one minute in the afternoon, be in thanks. Find at least one thing you can be truly grateful for and dwell on your good fortune. This should bring a smile to you. Find details to focus your gratitude. If you are thinking of how grateful you are for one or more of your children, think about some of the things they've done and said that make you feel particularly grateful. If you have an opportunity to express your gratitude to others, all the better. In fact, you can thank someone for some favor and now you've doubled down on gratitude and service, killing two birds with one grateful stone. One minute of thanks twice on Tuesday gives you a great perspective for whatever challenges the week holds for you.

Wednesday. Challenge day. For one minute in the morning and one minute in the afternoon, focus on challenge. You have some options here. You can choose to focus on a current challenge and think of what you are gaining and learning by taking it on. You can think of the discipline and the resourcefulness this challenge requires of you. You could also think of a past challenge and what it meant to you. What you learned. Perhaps you need to reevaluate your response. Maybe the passage of time has given you a new perspective on an earlier disappointment or triumph. This is your opportunity to remind yourself of the liberating thought that everything is designed for your benefit. Your midweek minute of focus on the challenges of your life will give you the healthy perspective on challenges that successful people have. You will respond to new challenges with a sense of welcome and a "can do" attitude. As this approach becomes a pillar of your identity, you will enjoy a sense of power that prevents you from becoming rattled as you may have been in the past.

Thursday. Ownership day. For one minute in the morning and one minute in the afternoon, focus on ownership. You are focusing on owning the results that are showing up in your life, not necessarily the possessions that you own. If you've worked to earn the income to buy something you value then you can focus on having created that result for yourself. But beyond that, there's a wealth of other things to consider, such as your relationships. Think about owning the way the important people in your life respond to you. If their response is not what you would like it to be, consider what you will do to change it. Resist the impulse to blame people or circumstances for the results you experience. Recognize that blaming others gives them a power over your life that should be yours. Ownership is about taking responsibility. As this sense of ownership becomes part of your identity, your sense of power will grow exponentially. You'll be right where you need to be in order to get the life you want.

Friday. Happy day. For one minute in the morning and one minute in the afternoon, you're going to be HAPPY! At a minimum, you've got to break a smile. If necessary, stick a pencil across your teeth, bite down and . . . smile. But you really need to go for a good laugh here. You can call a friend with a great sense of humor with a goal of finding something to laugh about, or you can think of something or someone who really makes you happy. If you don't feel all that happy on a given Friday, you may need to get creative, and this may be a bit of a challenge, but you've already addressed your attitude on challenges on Wednesday, so you'll be fine. I made it easy by setting this for Friday because we've been trained to think that all days are not created equal and that weekends are special. But once you redefine your identity, you'll come to appreciate that all days were meant to be enjoyed and it's up to you to do so.

Saturday. In-the-moment day. For one minute in the morning and one minute in the afternoon, you're going to "be." Your assignment is to simply feel whatever you're feeling. Whether this is good or bad is not the point. The point is that whatever it is, it absolutely is. And you are in the moment, experiencing your consciousness. You are aware. And what you are aware of is "now." For this minute, there is no past and no future, no beginning and no end, no winners and no losers. The beauty of this is that as long as you pay attention, you can't "get it wrong." Your thoughts may jump around as usual while you experience your surroundings, but you'll be aware of this, and this awareness of just being in the "now" will begin to revisit you regularly throughout the rest of the week.

Sunday. Review and plan day. For one minute in the morning you're going to review, and for one minute in the afternoon you're going to plan. For your review, think about how you did with your daily minutes. Did you have a particularly good laugh on Friday? Did you feel particularly good about helping someone on Monday? Are these sixty-second focus sessions starting to redefine who you are?

Is the awareness of directing your focus this way beginning to bleed over into the other minutes of your day? Do you find yourself assessing more consciously your responses to challenges? Do you find yourself taking more ownership for your life? Have you stopped blaming others for things that don't turn out the way you wanted? Look for at least one good memory to acknowledge and build on.

For your plan minute in the afternoon, you may think about what you want to accomplish this week and/or this year. If you are thinking about a long-term goal, you can back it up to this week and think about what you can do this week to move you toward that goal. And you can look ahead to service day on Monday, and think about who you will serve and how. You can think about the challenges and the joy ahead. You can visualize a good result to come by just "seeing" things go well. Your review and plan day will internalize your recent gains and set you up for more to come.

This is a weekly schedule that works key characteristics for your identity. Each time you complete a single sixty-second session, you will have exercised your ability to assert control over your consciousness in a way some people never do. You are intended to be a primary force in the universe and now you are living up to that promise.

Once you've established yourself with this, there are variations you can run as needed. Let's say you are having an issue with anxiety about a meeting you have to have or a test you have to take. You could take your afternoon session on a given day and simply visualize, or imaginize, a comfortable experience and a great result. This would be a natural point of focus for your challenge day, but if you feel the urge to make an adjustment on another day of the week, an afternoon substitution can let you address this.

Another empowering use of this focus challenge is what I call the mad-minute model. If you haven't already guessed, I'm a big fan of alliteration, a series of words that start with an identical sound. Snappy and memorable. We all have people we admire, people whose character we seek to emulate. We can model them for a minute, alone or with others. This is an "act as if" activity. We act as if we are that person, regardless of the circumstances we are in. We all "played" as others when we were young, cowboys or captains, princesses or teachers. There's no rule that you had to give this up when you turned thirteen. You can choose someone you've never met or a character from a film. Stand as they would stand, walk as they would walk, and act as they would act. And unless the person has an accent or some unique characteristic, you can take this on in a social setting without anyone realizing you're playing. Choose characters with the type of power you seek to exercise and play it.

The 7/60 Mad Minute Identity Design Plan is designed to serve as an ongoing link between the concepts of identity design and your everyday life. The importance of this can't be overstated because if you simply read this book and do the activities without reinforcing these concepts, you'll likely see these concepts fade as your standard patterns reassert themselves. **This is daily**

reinforcement geared to drive effective identity design. Mad minutes are 60 second action steps.

Prior to your encounter with this identity design program you've had years to develop your identity and the way you look at things. If you're going to redesign and redefine, if you're going to rewrite the patterns you've developed over the years, you're going to need to be engaged in an ongoing reinforcement program. This is mad. This is your mad minute. What are you waiting for?

○⊂⊃ POINTS TO REMEMBER: ⊂⊃○

- People with a plan make things happen. Would you rather be the pinball or the pinball wizard?
- If you think you're too busy to plan, the fact is you're too busy not to.
- If you're not shooting for something . . . you're shooting for nothing.
- When setting your goals, state your outcome in positive terms, be specific, and state a measurable result.
- Direction is more important than placement. We are always on the journey.
- We don't need a "to do" list. We need a "to win" list.
- Time is a zero-sum game. Thus, we need a "not to do" list.
- The 7/60 Mad Minute Plan is identity design for busy people. Start now.
- The 7/60 Mad Minute Identity Design Plan is designed to serve as an ongoing link between the concepts of identity design and your everyday life. This is daily reinforcement geared to drive effective identity design.

THE NOW IDENTITY

*There's something about death that is comforting. The thought
that you could die tomorrow frees you to appreciate your life now.*
—Angelina Jolie

Now and then it's good to pause in our pursuit of happiness and just be happy.
—Guillaume Apollinaire

*Happiness is the only good. The time to be happy is now. The place
to be happy is here. The way to be happy is to make others so.*
—Robert Green Ingersoll

*There are only two days of the year you can't get anything done.
One is called yesterday and the other is called tomorrow.*
—The Dalai Lama

M y three favorite times of the year? Now, now, and NOW! Think of how beautiful life would be if everyone lived in the now—if people didn't spend all their time dragging the baggage of their past around, and cycling their vague hopes and fears about the future, but actually lived right now. Not this morning or this evening, earlier or later, or even a minute ago, or a minute from now, but right now! After all, isn't it the only time we have real control over? When you really wrap yourself around this, when you Velcro yourself to this, it's so damn liberating . . . it's intoxicating.

What is your greatest resource? What's the one thing that most influences everything else about your life? Would it be your income, your possessions, your relationships, your intelligence, your fitness, your experience? All of these things play a part in your life, but there's one thing that is an overriding influence on all of these things. There's one thing that determines how significant any of these things really are. There's one resource that you can train yourself to control. There's one resource you can discipline yourself to achieve maximum benefit. So, what do you think? List your most valuable resource. DO THIS NOW.

There may be various responses that speak to the same basic answer. What is your greatest resource? Your attention. Attention, your attention, is something you can and will own with some practice. And owning your attention will give you more control over your life than anything else. Managing your attention allows you to shape your attitude. Once you train your attention and shape your attitude, the rest of the world belongs to you. Your perception of the world becomes a joystick that you control at will. You own the world. **Again, your greatest resource is your attention.**

If you're not happy right now, it's because of where you've put your attention. The greatest resource any of us has to change our mood is the ability to shift our attention from one thought to another. What is the greatest skill anyone can develop?

What is the one skill shown to make you healthier, wealthier, more powerful, productive and popular, more confident, content, cooperative, constructive and creative, more flexible, generous and grateful, more energetic, engaging and resilient, and more loving?

Happiness. Do you want more of all of the above? If you want to be happier, you need to pay attention to where you are paying attention. Pay attention to happy, and get happy. Pay attention to sad, and get sad. Pay attention to mad . . . and . . . you get the idea. You need to take responsibility for how happy you are in the same way you need to take ownership of the rest of your life. If you suffer from HDD (Happiness Deficit Disorder), you're not paying enough attention to things that make you happy.

As we noted earlier, the happiest people are not the richest, or the prettiest, or the smartest, or the strongest people in the world. They're the most giving. They're also the people who are the best at paying attention to the things that make and keep them happy. They're good at thinking about things that they are grateful for that they already have, rather than coveting what their neighbor has. They're good at spending time with people they love and expressing their love. They're good at living in the moment and paying attention to whatever is good about the moment. They're good at forgiving, and they're good at giving and living. They are especially good at giving. They see giving as having meaning.

And they're great at connecting. The reason they're so great at connecting is that they see and feel themselves connected to others. They look for the good in the people around them, and they are always acknowledging this. While they realize that people have faults, they don't dwell on them. They know what they are looking for, and acknowledging the good in people makes themselves and everyone around them feel better and feel happier. Being around happy people is even more reason to be . . . happy.

We can now see how some of these concepts tie together and become what can be referred to as the Power Identity Triangle. The first corner of the triangle is giving, or service. We have discussed at length the beauty and the power and the importance of giving. We have looked at the fact that giving leads to a greater sense of fulfillment and meaning. Giving people are happier, and the more people give, the happier they are.

This increased happiness, as a result of the giving, creates the second corner of the triangle, the happiness corner. We have also discussed the fact that happiness is the ultimate skill because when we are happier, we are more confident, more powerful. We are better at virtually everything we do. And we've discussed the many benefits of happiness at length too. This leads to the third corner of the triangle, the power corner. So, giving leads to happiness, and happiness leads to power, and once you have more power, you have more to give. And you can continue to cycle around the triangle with increased power and momentum. So, our Power Identity Triangle can be represented like this:

Happiness

Giving   Power

There is the question of NOW. If you could look at a list of all of the thoughts that crossed your mind in a given day, how many do you think would be precisely tuned to the exact moment they appear? How many would be now thoughts? Write out as many thoughts as you can think of in a two-minute period and see how many reflect your ability to be in the present. DO THIS NOW.

When we spend our time looking in the rearview mirror (thinking of our past), or thinking about what is around the next bend, we miss what is all around us. The past and the present don't exist now. The past is only what we remember. It's only what's in our head. That doesn't mean it didn't happen, but it's not here now. You can't wrap your hands around it. It's not here anymore. As for the future, you can't wrap your hands around that either. It's not here. Learn from the past. Yes. Plan for the future. Yes. But don't live in the past or the future. That's not where the power is. Research has indicated that we are not thinking of what we're doing; we're not "present" an average of 47 percent of the time.

Where is the best place to be? When is the best time to be there? Here and now! When you answer "Here and now," you open the door to the best of the real joy and challenges of life. No other answer gets you any closer to reality because it's where and when you are. When you start seeing here and now as your perfect place and time, and you start living here and now, you begin to understand what it means to "have it all" because you begin to live with all that you have. While this might sound clever and appear illusory, the fact is it's very real. And there's nothing quite like living joyfully in the real world.

What's the matter with now? The problem with now is . . . there is no problem. Repeat: The problem with now is there's no problem . . . but we often don't recognize that there isn't one. The fact is now will give us whatever we bring to it. We can choose what to pay attention to now, and what we choose to pay attention to will define our now. And if you see a problem with now, then look inside, because whatever it is, it is within you. And you are the one who gets to decide to move your attention from one thought to another.

In his book *The Social Animal*, David Brooks discusses the concept of attention with an interesting analogy. A newborn child's attention is like the light of a lantern; it's diffuse and constantly shifting with anything that enters its field of vision. There's no real sense of "self-direction," and a child's world is governed by its surroundings. As we mature, we gain the ability to direct our focus, and the more mature we are, the more control we can exert over our focus. We are no longer a lantern spilling the light of our attention in every direction, but more of a flashlight, and the most focused among us are lasers, able to zero in on a line of thought and apply our concentration in a dedicated way. The concept of flow, which we discussed earlier, is a beautiful example of "laser" focus, a place in our mind, a manner of thought in which nothing else matters. When we think of our attention as our greatest resource, we can think of our ability to control it, to "mine" it, to manage it, in spite of distractions, as our golden ticket to the life we want.

If you think back to the members of the Youth Deterrent Team, who I introduced at the beginning of this book, they are a great example of the kind of "attention management" that makes life meaningful. Serving a life sentence in prison gives anyone a load of negatives to think about. Yet, these individuals focus on steering young people away from the choices they made when they were young. Every aspect of our lives is determined by how we manage our attention.

The beauty of now, and the ability to be "present," is a rare and invaluable skill that pays immediate and ongoing dividends. Our ability to be present is a direct reflection of our ability to manage our attention. Once we master the ability to manage our attention, we essentially control our world. This leads us directly to the life we want because we create our life as we lead it. Internal focus overrules external circumstances every time.

Many will say, "My mind is always talking. Thoughts are always 'coming at me,' and it's like being in a flood or a windstorm. It's not something that I can control." The best tonic for dealing with this flood and getting present that I have found is to meditate. Meditation manages the flood and disciplines our mind. This is a critical skill. I learned Transcendental Meditation in 2010 and have practiced it daily since then. I had tried various forms of meditation, including working with recordings that were intended to assist me in achieving deep meditative states.

Nothing stuck until I learned Transcendental Meditation. I've come to learn that not all forms of meditation are created equal.

TM, as it's known, is effortless and has been taught to children and adults of all ages all across the globe. The fact is it works. It quiets the mind, and it has improved every aspect of my life. Personally, the level of control I'm able to exercise over all the mental issues that I've talked about in this program has been immeasurably improved by my meditation practice. I'm calmer and more centered than ever. If something upsetting happens, I'm able to self-regulate or regroup quicker than ever. And I'm considerably happier to boot.

My meditation instructor was Farrokh Anklesaria. I found him on the Internet when I was told about his program, The Enlightened Sentencing Project, in St. Louis. I called him up, and after hearing him discuss the success he was having teaching meditation to adults who had been sentenced to probation for their crimes, I told him it all sounded too good to be true. He invited me to come to St. Louis, to teach me to meditate and to introduce me to the judges who referred him cases and to some of the graduates of his program.

In February of 2010, I took him up on this offer and flew to St. Louis for four days. During my first meditation session with Farrokh, I felt a deep sense of relaxation. It felt like I was floating in nothing. It was a life altering experience. Farrokh also introduced me to two of his graduates. These were individuals with multiple felonies and histories of drug abuse that included alcohol as well as multiple substances. They told me they had faked their way through every rehab program they had been enrolled in before participating in The Enlightened Sentencing Project. Farrokh didn't ask them why they were there or what they had done wrong. He just taught them to meditate, and they credited their complete turnaround to their meditation practice. One was now a college English professor. These were compelling testimonials, and I resolved to add TM instruction to the services available to the young people adjudicated in our court.

The mental and physical benefits of TM are well documented in over 300 peer-reviewed research papers. Individuals who struggle with issues of poor school performance, impulse control, abandonment, self-esteem, mental health, and criminal behavior can all benefit from TM. A recent study stated that veterans who practiced TM showed a 50 percent reduction in symptoms of post-traumatic stress (PTS).

Some of San Francisco's worst performing schools have been transformed by the Quiet Time program in which the whole school learns to meditate and does so daily. Research data shows an 85 percent reduction in school suspensions and a 65 percent reduction in school violence over two years. Stress, anxiety, and depression were all reduced significantly. Students reported greater self-confidence, focus, and happiness. James S. Dierke, the executive vice president of the American Federation of School Administrators, calls the Quiet Time program the most powerful, effective program he's seen in his forty-year public school career.

None of this is the least bit surprising to me, given my personal experience with TM. I practice daily and will continue to do so. TM gives me a better grasp of the moment than I've ever had. So, TM can give you better access to being in the moment too. Information on TM instruction is available at TM.org.

The now we have is the now we create. If we don't like it, it's up to us to create a new one. That's the beauty of now. Our now is full of power; we just need to exercise it. Our now lets us acknowledge where we are AND where we are going! As long as we're willing to recognize that our journey is where the action is, rather than our destination, then we're exactly where we need to be. We have exactly what we need. If we've never realized this, now would be a great time for that too!

And that's another great thing about now: We may not have some things that we "want," but we do have what we need. Our attention and our direction are our choice, and any failure to recognize this means we're not paying attention to what we're paying attention to. If this seems somewhat circular, that our identity now shapes what we're thinking about, and what we're thinking about is shaping our identity and who we are at this very moment . . . that's because . . . it is!

Every thought we have has an effect on who we are. It becomes part of our experience. Who we are affects the thoughts we have and where we focus our attention. While this all has a circular quality to it, that doesn't mean you can't impact it. You can! Everything we've discussed here is geared to allow you to do just that.

And that's what makes now so powerful. Problems may persist, but now remains what we make it, regardless. **Now is like the fairytale story "Beauty and the Beast." It's what we choose to see, the beauty or the beast.**

Yesterday is gone and tomorrow is promised to no one, so that leaves us with . . . you guessed it . . . now. It's really all we have at this moment, so why not make the best of it? As we do, we make the best of ourselves.

If you still feel there is a problem with now, I recommend you make that problem as small as possible because, frankly, it's impeding your progress. It's bringing you down. You want to develop your ability to savor the moment. How well can you savor?

If you're going to effectively live in the now, you're going to have to be present. When you are present, so many things open up for you. Here are some specific benefits you can look for when you are really present:

When you are present, you are more spontaneous and creative. You are more open, and this makes you able to see more options wherever you are. Spontaneity is an immediate reaction. When you are already present, you don't have to pull yourself into the present to be spontaneous. You're already there!

When you are present, you have the ability to shrink big jobs into small ones. How? You can only work one moment at a time. Look at it this way, how much can you do in a moment? Maybe not much. But then, that's all you have to do in that moment, all that you can.

A great time to practice this ability to be present is during any fitness workout. There may be a tendency to think about how long and hard your workout is going to be. Better to just focus on what you're doing each moment of the workout and the fact that it's good to be doing what you're doing. It's work, for sure, but that's what you're there for.

Even when we're under a deadline, we can concentrate on what we can get done in the moment we're in. What more can we do? We need to make sure we have an adequate plan for whatever our project or task is. If not, we may need to take time to plan, but once we do then we can just pay attention to what we're doing to get the job done. How does a marathon runner run a race? All the runners who have ever competed, and all the champions who have ever won a race, run a race in the same way. One step at a time!

Being present profoundly changes the experience of eating. Previously, we discussed the fact that you can't watch TV and be present to your eating. This divides your attention. It's recommended that you chew each bite forty times. When you do this, if you're like me, this completely changes the experience of eating. While

I don't usually count now, once you've done this, you realize how much you're missing when you just gobble down your food without paying attention to eating.

When your food is good, you get the most out of it by fully chewing it. If your food is not good, you may find you just can't eat things that you otherwise would. This can pay real dividends for you as you eliminate things like fast food from your diet. Eating good food should be a regular and special part of your day. You need to be present and to pay attention. Don't expect much in the way of nutrition if you "eat and run." Eat and run? That's a bad combination. Eat and savor, much better, no comparison.

When you are present, you learn more and you deepen your understanding. Whether you're working on a skill, such as in sports or music, or you're reading, or listening or watching to acquire new information, being fully present is the best state to be in. You appreciate subtleties and may find yourself forming metaphors for whatever it is you're working on or learning.

When you are present, you perform better. Performance is a function of preparation and concentration. **Being present optimizes performance at everything.** You can't expect to perform well if you're not paying attention to what you're doing. In a survey of twenty-two activities, the one activity in which most people reported being present the most was sex. This alone may be the best indicator of how valuable it is to be present.

In competitive sports, the most common observation that's made when a player misplays a play during a game is that they lost focus. In other words, their performance dropped off because they got distracted, and at the moment, they weren't fully paying attention to what they were doing. Entertainers, teachers, and speakers need to be present to connect with their audience. If they're not present, it won't matter how prepared they are, they simply won't be able to connect effectively.

When you are present, you are less attracted to passive entertainment like TV. David Cain, who writes for his website Raptitude.com, discusses this in his article on the benefits of being present.

When you are in the moment, you might still choose to watch something, but bad TV, like bad food, is not something you are as likely to settle for when you're present. You realize you have better things to do. The benefits of not watching worthless programming are substantial because it actually buys us time that we otherwise waste. Who couldn't use more time?

Mr. Cain points out some additional great benefits of being present.

When you are present, you release the burdens of debts and obligations and any other concerns that are separate from what you are working on at the moment. Your long-term worries and pressures have no meaning in the present. Logically, there's no sense in worrying about these things if you're not working on them at the moment. This alone may be the biggest benefit of being present. We have an entertainment industry with music, movies, comedy, theatre, sports, and more designed to allow us to escape our worries. Yet, rather than escape from life and our worries, simply being present allows us to escape into life, into the world where we really exist. The better we are able to do this, the less we need the escapism of the entertainment industry.

When you are present, you are not preoccupied with your appearance or what others are thinking about you. You become less self-obsessed. By being conscious and present you become less self-conscious, especially in all the ways that are negative.

When you are present, you connect. Your ability to connect with anyone you meet, or anyone you are with, is greatest when you are present. You bond quicker and deeper. You understand others better. You empathize more. You're better company.

Being present is a skill. The better you are, the more you benefit. So, how present are you? Are you experiencing the benefits listed here? One way to get in touch with this is to review your mindset daily, or even hourly, until you get in touch with the skill of being present. Ask yourself how present you were to whatever you were doing for the last hour. Ask yourself how well you've done. What could you have done better? What could you have done more joyfully? The more you do this, the more you position yourself to experience the benefits of being present.

The science fiction film *Live Die Repeat* presents a storyline that touches on a number of the themes discussed here. In the film, the planet Earth is under attack by alien invaders who have the ability to manipulate the fabric of time and reset time by going back so they can adjust their actions based on any defensive measures taken by the earthlings. Tom Cruise, who plays the lead character, Lt. Col. Cage, is wounded and infected with the blood of the aliens, so he acquires this ability to return in time to the moment he wakes up after receiving his injury. His return in time is triggered each time he dies, thus the title, *Live Die Repeat*. Each time he dies, he has the knowledge of everything he learned up until the time of his death, including all the actions of the aliens. This gives him the knowledge to learn from his mistakes and adapt new countermeasures each time he "repeats."

This is a classic example of learning by doing, of learning by doing what doesn't work. In the film, each time Cage does something that doesn't work, he dies and "starts over." Our mistakes don't "kill" us, but there's no reason we can't use our mistakes exactly the way Lt. Col. Cage uses his in the film.

When the film starts, he is a soldier in name only. He lacks any combat experience and wants nothing to do with being sent into battle. Each time he starts over, he does so with more and more confidence. By the end of the film, he is brimming with the take-command bravado that is a trademark of the characters we're accustomed to seeing Tom Cruise play. It's a powerful personal transformation. In one scene, when he is wounded and realizes he will not be able to complete his mission, he invites his colleague to finish him off, to kill him so he can make a fresh start with what he has learned to that point.

You can watch this film and think of yourself and the mistakes you've made and what you've learned from them. Think of your personal growth spurred on as you move beyond each mistake or mishap. Think of how each day you can build upon everything you've learned and experienced from the day before. Model the character transformation and the supercharged confidence of Lt. Col. Cage in the film.

It has been a pleasure to share these thoughts with you. I'm struck by the fact that I've probably learned more by writing this book than anyone can learn from reading it. Whether that's true, if it merely leads you to consciously take on the task of deciding who you want to be, and of designing your identity, who you are, you'll be rewarded in so many ways that it will be impossible to keep track. And, as you may know by now, finding things that are impossible is a challenge for me.

Your productivity, your success, your happiness are all within your hands . . . now. In fact, they have always been. One of the reasons you may never have seen this is that, frankly, very few people do. We are busy. We are distracted. We are not present much of the time. We are not paying attention to the things we are paying attention to, and we don't realize how important this is. Now is the time to change all of this.

It is all a matter of perception, and when you change the way you look at things, the things you look at change. Your life changes. You don't have to "take" things in your hands, just feel what's already there. Some may think this is hard to do. But is it? How hard is it to pay attention to your thoughts?

If it's not what you're used to, you will find you'll get better at this every time you think of it. And this is how it is with every concept covered here. The more you think about being grateful, the more grateful you will be. The more you think about the things that make you happy, the happier you'll be. The happier you are, the more productive, and creative, and spontaneous, and successful, and connected you'll be. And these things in turn will make you even happier. There's never been a better time to do this than now.

For our final act here, I leave you with this declaration for your direct empowerment. Recite this daily for thirty days, or whatever amount of time it may take you to assimilate this truth.

The DFB (Declaration of Freedom to Be) or the PEP (Personal Emancipation Proclamation)

I, _____, do hereby declare that I am not defined by what I have. I am not defined by where I live, what I drive, or what I wear. I am not defined by what I have done or what I have failed to do. I am not defined by what people say or think about me.

I, _____, am solely defined by my personal vision, and I hereby declare my freedom from any limits to that vision. I acknowledge my power to be whoever I choose to be, to be as brave, or generous, or strong, or great, good or bad, as I choose to be. I acknowledge the power and the responsibility to design my identity to live the life of my dreams. From this moment forward, I and only I, shall be responsible for my identity. I shall think what I choose to think. I shall do what I choose to do. I shall be who I choose to be. I AM FREE.

○⊂⊃ POINTS TO REMEMBER: ⊂⊃○

- My three favorite times of the year? Now, now, and NOW!
- Your greatest resource is your attention.
- The now we have is the now we create. If we don't like it, it's up to us to create a new one.
- Now is like the fairytale story of "Beauty and the Beast." It's what we choose to see, the beauty or the beast.
- Being present profoundly changes the experience of eating.
- Being present optimizes performance at everything.
- Being present is a skill. The better you are, the more you benefit.
- Your productivity, your success, your happiness are all within your hands . . . now. In fact, they have always been.
- Where is the best place to be? When is the best time? Here and now!

APPENDIX
IDENTITY DESIGN 49 QUESTIONNAIRE

Identity has been defined as a sense of self or the distinct personality of an individual. True or false, circle one. Fill in the blanks as indicated.

1. I believe in justice for all. An injustice to any person is harmful to me and to our community.   T F
2. I believe in treating other people the way I like to be treated.   T F
3. I'm excited about what I'm doing and where I'm heading.   T F
4. I believe I need to be more in control than I am now.   T F
5. I believe I am alive with the intention that I be productive, successful, and happy.   T F
6. I believe some people have an unfair advantage in life.   T F
7. My beliefs regarding the statement above in # 6 have an effect on my ability to be productive, successful, and happy.   T F
8. I believe my sense of identity can be influenced by many factors.   T F
9. A major factor influencing my identity is what I own.   T F
10. Self-acceptance is more important than self-improvement.   T F
11. I am responsible for the way that people respond to me.   T F

12. I have a difficult time facing challenges.   T F

13. Possessions mean more to me when I want them than when I have them.
T F

14. My happiness depends more on the way I look than how I feel.   T F

15. When I have a problem, it helps to complain about it.   T F

16. I am more effective when I am angry.   T F

17. When I experience failure or a disappointment, it is easier for me to control what I do than to control what I feel.   T F

18. When I change what I'm doing, it generally changes what I'm thinking.
T F

19. I have a personal plan to improve myself that includes specific activities that I do at least once a week.   T F

20. I like to learn by (circle any that apply):
reading   listening   watching   doing

21. Being accepted by others means a lot to me.   T F

22. I tend to "follow the crowd."   T F

23. I have a habit of complaining about things that I don't control, like the weather.   T F

24. No one can embarrass me without my permission.   T F

25. I may not always have what I want, but I have what I need and I don't worry about money.   T F

26. What I think about does not generally affect my health.   T F

27. When I disagree with someone, I do my best to understand their point of view.   T F

28. In school or at work, I generally do just enough to get by.   T F

29. The events and circumstances of my life are specifically designed for my benefit.   T F

30. When I have a difficult decision to make, it helps if I can distract myself and think of something else for a while before making up my mind.
T F

31. When I do something for someone, I generally expect something in return.
T F

32. I have a difficult time admitting my mistakes.   T F

33. I take more pride in what I accomplish based on my talent than in what I accomplish based on my effort.　　T　F

34. Habits are responsible for about 40 percent of what I do.　　T　F

35. I tend to spend more time thinking about what has happened and what will happen than being present and in the moment.　　T　F

36. I generally recognize when I need help, and I ask for it.　　T　F

37. The person most responsible for my identity is

_____

38. The person I receive the most support from is

_____

39. A strength of mine is

_____

40. One thing I'd like to change about my behavior is

_____

_____

41. I will be happy when I

_____

_____

42. If I could have a superpower, I would like to be able to

_____

_____

43. One of the best things anyone ever did for me was

_____

_____

44. If my life ended today, I would be remembered as someone who

_____

_____

_____

45. At the end of my life, I would like to be able to say that I

_____

_____

_____

46. One of my happiest moments was when I

_____

_____

_____

_____

47. I feel I am in control when I

_____

_____

_____

_____

48. I believe I can redefine myself by changing my beliefs.   T   F
49. I am loved. My best days are ahead.   T   F

BIBLIOGRAPHY

These are books you should be reading. It is critical to be proactive about designing your identity. We are flooded with messages on a daily basis from a mix of sources, many of which, frankly, are not very helpful or are downright destructive to the development of the commanding identity we need in order to get the life we want.

We can counter this trend by working to surround ourselves with positive people and minimizing negative contacts. One of the best things we can do is to read from the works of some of the greatest thinkers in the field of personal development. You have these works at your fingertips, no farther than your local library. These are guidelines, great ideas for productive and joyful living, and you can't afford not to have them. And once you have them, you can't afford not to use them. Make it a point to regularly read something to improve your character. You should be reading something at least once a month, if not weekly.

Reading these books is like sitting down with the author and having a conversation in which they tell you what they consider to be the most important ideas regarding the business of living. A good starting point is the list below. These authors are leaders in the field.

I am living the life of my dreams due in a large part to what I've learned and the support I've had from my parents, my family, and friends, and from a personal desire to "be all I can be." But I'd be kidding myself if I didn't acknowledge the debt

I owe to the pioneers of personal development. Trailblazers like Dale Carnegie, Norman Vincent Peale, and Anthony Robbins have written books and created programs that have helped millions. When I first discovered these books, it was a revelation. Jack Canfield and Mark Victor Hansen mastered the use of stories to touch the lives of millions.

Biographies of great achievers are also highly recommended. A good biography gives you an inside look into the thought process of a person's life. Biographies introduce you to role models. There's no reason you shouldn't learn from the life of someone, even if they died long before you were born.

Recommendations

Allen, David. *Getting Things Done: How to Achieve Stress-free Productivity*. New York: Simon and Schuster, 2008.

Anderson, Walter. *The Confidence Course*. New York: HarperCollins, 1997.

Bossidy, Larry and Ram Charan. *Execution: The Discipline of Getting Things Done*. New York: Crown Business, 2002.

Canfield, Jack with Janet Switzer. *The Success Principles*. Glasgow: Collins, 2007. (Note: Page 358 includes a story of personal acknowledgment about my father, the first Judge Frank Szymanski. Now, there was a man to be reckoned with: Raised seven children, all college graduates, with my mother, Lillian; won a national football championship with Notre Dame and another with the Philadelphia Eagles after being a first round NFL draft choice; bought and paid for the Mackinac Bridge as the Auditor General of the State of Michigan (well, his name was on the checks!); worked on the atomic bomb, the Manhattan Project as a student at Notre Dame with one of his professors assigned to the project; served as a trial judge for twenty-seven years; developed friendships and helped people from all walks of life without limit to race, creed, national origin, or economic or social status; and, in marrying my mother, partnered with someone of equal power, influence, faith, and humility.)

Brooks, David. *The Social Animal: The Hidden Sources of Love, Character, and Achievement*. New York: Random House, 2011.

Bronson, Po and Ashley Merryman. *NurtureShock: New Thinking about Children*. New York: Twelve Books, 2009.

Carnegie, Dale. *How to Stop Worrying and Start Living*. New York: Pocket Books, 2004.

Carnegie, Dale. *How to Win Friends and Influence People*. New York: Simon and Schuster, 2009.

Carlson, Richard. *Don't Sweat the Small Stuff — And It's All Small Stuff*. New York: Hyperion, 1997.

Carson, Ben. *Think Big*. Grand Rapids: Zondervan Publishing House, 1993.

Chandler, Steve. *The Joy of Selling*. Bandon: Robert D. Reed Publishers, 2010.

Chopra, Deepak. *The Seven Spiritual Laws of Success*. San Rafael: Amber-Allen Publishing, 2007.

Chopra, Deepak. *Ageless Body, Timeless Mind*. New York: Harmony Books, 1993.

Coyle, Daniel. *The Talent Code: Greatness Isn't Born. It's Grown. Here's How*. New York: Bantam, 2009.

Covey, Sean. *The 7 Habits of Highly Effective Teens*. New York: Fireside Books, 1998.

Covey, Stephen R. *The 7 Habits of Highly Effective People*. New York: Simon and Schuster, 1989.

Covey, Stephen R. *First Things First*. New York: Simon and Schuster, 1994.

Csikszentmihalyi, Mihaly. *Flow: The Psychology of Optimal Experience*. New York: Harper and Row, 1990.

Glasser, William. *Control Theory*. New York: Harper and Row, 1984.

Goleman, Daniel. *Emotional Intelligence*. New York: Bantam Books, 1995.

Goleman, Daniel. *Social Intelligence*. New York: Bantam Books, 2006.

Hill, Napoleon. *Think and Grow Rich*. Greenwich: Fawcett Publications, 1960.

Kawasaki, Guy. *Enchantment: The Art of Changing Hearts, Minds and Actions*. London: Portfolio Penguin, 2011.

Lyubomirsky, Sonja. *The How of Happiness: A Scientific Approach to Getting the Life You Want*. New York: Penguin, 2007.

Murphy, Joseph. *The Power of Your Subconscious Mind*. Englewood Cliffs: Prentice-Hall, 1963.

Myers, David G. *The Pursuit of Happiness: Who is Happy, and Why?* New York: Harper Paperbacks, 1993.

Neill, Michael. *You Can Have What You Want: Proven Strategies for Inner and Outer Success*. Carlsbad: Hay House, Inc., 2006.

Parrott, Les and Neil Clark Warren. *Love the Life You Live*. Wheaton: Tyndale House Publishers, 2003.

Peale, Norman Vincent. *The Power of Positive Thinking*. New York: Fireside/Simon and Schuster, 2003.

Pearsall, Paul. *The Pleasure Principle*. Alameda: Hunter House Publishers, 1996.

Pearsall, Paul. *Super Joy: In Love with Living*. New York: Doubleday, 1988.

Prentiss, Chris. *Be Who You Want, Have What You Want: Change Your Thinking, Change Your Life*. Los Angeles: Power Press, 2008.

Roazzi, Vincent M. *The Spirituality of Success*. Dallas: Brown Books, 2002.

Robbins, Anthony. *Unlimited Power*. New York: Simon and Schuster, 1986.

Robbins, Anthony. *Awaken the Giant Within*. New York: Summit Books, 1991.

Seligman, Martin E. P. *Authentic Happiness: Using the New Positive Psychology to Realize Your Potential for Lasting Fulfillment*. New York: Free Press, 2002.

Schwartz, David J. *The Magic of Thinking Big*. New York: Simon and Schuster, 2007.

Tolle, Eckhart. *The Power of Now*. Novato: New World Library, 2002.

Weinzweig, Ari. *Zingerman's Guide to Giving Great Service*. New York: Hyperion, 2004.

Wiseman, Richard. *59 Seconds: Think a Little, Change a Lot*. New York: Alfred A. Knopf, 2009.

Printed in the USA
CPSIA information can be obtained
at www.ICGtesting.com
JSHW080031161123
52157JS00005B/258

9 781630 474355